Rethinking AI

Grace Iordanov

NEWMAN SPRINGS PUBLISHING
320 Broad Street
Red Bank, NJ 07701

First originally published by Newman Springs Publishing 2024

ISBN 979-8-89308-642-3 (Paperback)
ISBN 979-8-89308-643-0 (Digital)

Printed in the United States of America

Contents

Introduction

AI and Our Fears

Today's world is full of AI, from ChatGPT to Midjourney, an AI you can ask to create a customized image for you in any great aesthetic or to solve a tough question you have been pondering for weeks. AI is becoming more and more embedded in our everyday lives, and while it is not clear how much more or for how long it will continue to advance and improve, a major block is in our way of this process. From a recent poll, 67 percent of correspondents have stated that they are worried about where AI developments are going and if you just look on MSN news any article about AI it is almost surely to be portraying AI in a negative light, whether it is mentioning the newest development in the field.

AI is one of the most hated pieces of technology around the world. Many people fear AI taking their jobs or becoming the real Terminator, but AI is not as grim as it may first seem. Surely AI is not very widely understood and is complex to even many trained professionals, but AI is an important asset to the world, and very little of what is being said in the media is true about it. Movies for years have been made based on "what-if" scenarios for new developments in AI. What if a new superhuman robot is created that can destroy the world accidentally? What happens if an enemy in warfare gets hold of this technology and uses it before the other side? The notion of AI being dangerous to humanity and a perfect weapon of mass destruction has become highly ingrained in our minds as being the inevitable trajectory of modern AI technologies and developments, but it isn't the only possibility.

AI has also made such a big positive impact on our lives that it becomes questionable what our lives would be like without this technology. Finding a great video online will become much more difficult, finding a great product online will become harder since you will not receive advertisements with products related to recent searches. Google uses AI to recommend content you might have never seen before but are otherwise interested in given your past search and browsing history. AI can be used to help people suffering from debilitating conditions be able to live more normal lives. AI is a tool that completes tasks that we otherwise don't take into account anymore. In a world becoming increasingly complex, it has become more important that we learn about how we can perform our daily tasks and make our lives easier, and this is what AI can help us accomplish.

We sometimes think of this world as being more complex than twenty years ago, but today, it is much easier than ever before. In the past, people were only able to travel by either ship or horse anywhere they wanted to go, and if they had to travel from Britain to the US, they had to travel by ship for weeks or months depending on the season and the wind patterns. An animal like a horse, which was often used for travel, would get tired and need to stop for a break and the experience of traveling on the back of it or in a shabby wagon led by it was highly uncomfortable. For centuries throughout history, humans have lived in this way, having to put immense physical and mental effort into something that today we would take for granted.

Today, if you want to travel between two very distant countries at the opposite ends of their continents, like Spain and China, you can just take a flight for twenty-one hours and thirty minutes with a comfortable seat and Wi-Fi. Travel has become much easier over time thanks to technological improvements, but it has not been the only major aspect of our lives to have been improved. Our way of doing math and making decisions has also improved rapidly too. Before calculators were invented, doing math was a very tedious job in any number system, such as the base ten system (a number system where we only have ten different digits: 0, 1, 2, 3, 4, 5, 6, 7, 8, 9) or binary (a number system where we only have two distinct digits: 1 and 0). We had to do by hand all operations by mathematics no matter how complex or long the task we needed to complete was. (There is a reason why many universities have sometimes sixteen whiteboards in the same room.) If a student who had learned how to do math without a calculator came into today's world, they would be hailed as a global young math prodigy for being able to do numerous complex operations in their head or doing all of them manually on paper without making a small mistake.

This may entail the question then of why we then would consider everything to be much more complex then it was before. The answer lies not within the improvements we have made but in how these improvements are used. We live in an abundance of innovations created by people over centuries up until this point, and yet people today simply don't know how to use them. We live with very modern technologies that are at our fingertips, but many people have not grown up with them and later need to adapt to using them. After Henry Ford invented the automobile for the average person, it took time for people to get used to driving to be able to go where they wanted to go. Today, the situation is similar with new technologies such as AI and computer software like Microsoft Word or Excel. These technologies are newer to us than cars or telephones. Therefore, unless you have actively used one of them for most of your life, you would not be as comfortable with using the technology as someone who has. But this does not have to be this way. The process can be faster if these new topics are explained in an easy way for a person who is not very familiar with the topic or a related one to understand it well enough to use it properly or even to discover more on their own about it.

AI has grown over the years into a very complex system that we perceive to be something comparable to an unearthly force when comparing it to technologies that we have used for many years before it, but we have at the same time gotten so used to this technology that we sometimes don't realize that we are even using it anymore for basic things such as doing paying for a new shirt we buy or driving to the city, and new AI developments can continue to automate more tedious and even dangerous tasks that humans should not be doing.

In today's media outlets, the outcome of AI progress is primarily being looked down upon as saturating the job market and making certain careers obsolete, but is this really the full picture? AI has the ability to bring many good outcomes along with many bad outcomes, just like any other technology. Back when IBM first developed a computer to aid the US government in tallying votes in a past presidential election, there were already concerns of the voting machines and powerful computers made for its time (such as those made by IBM) stealing 90 percent of jobs away from people. Fast-forward to today and the outcome of the new machines that IBM has developed during this time has led to only 8 percent of jobs from the 1950s being automated.

Today, people may think this as being different with more intelligent algorithms and computers with higher RAM for doing more calculations and more powerful algorithms such as Open AI's ChatGPT or Google's Bard, but these AI algorithms cannot perform many of the things that people in the media may say that they can perform. In fact, many of these algorithms still have difficulties performing simple tasks accurately. Take the simple task of drawing a circle, which a first-grade human who knows what the shape of a circle is can do with 85 percent accuracy, but when asked, ChatGPT can only draw a polygon in the shape of a circle with a few vertices. Even more complicated tasks that the media dubs that AI can perform at a higher level than a trained professional, AI can only perform at an amateur level or worse.

Think about it: if we have such an ultra-intelligent companion like a search on our web browser, why wouldn't we use it for difficult tasks that can give us high returns? If ChatGPT can perform better than the average Wall Street stock trader, why don't we all use ChatGPT for choosing stocks for our portfolios and become millionaires? Well, people of course have tried doing this, and the AI algorithms picked fairly good stocks, but did they beat the market by a long enough shot to rake in even over $100000? No. What about asking AI to code? Many software engineers have feared ever since the first version of ChatGPT came out of losing their jobs due to AI, but is it really possible for AI to code at the level of a developer?

Could it write as many lines of code that work as well in a certain environment as a developer can on their own?

If an AI algorithm were to accurately solve a complex bug within the software, it would need to write algorithms that can easily be integrated with the system in which the bug is in, but can it do that in a program with possibly millions of lines of code and multiple different files connected together in an entirely another desktop app? With today's AI algorithms such as ChatGPT and Bard AI accepting only a few lines of input, they cannot accept as input an entire 1,300-line code script in which the AI would need to process to understand the system to solve the bug. Also, when it comes to complex applications including many libraries in certain programming languages and many different files with code written in different languages the AI, it would be impossible for an AI program at today's level to debug the program. At best, in a more simple script, it would either fail to produce a well-working solution, or AI may not create a solution at all if it deems the prompt of the user too demanding and just provides as an answer a simple link to online documentation websites for the developer to look up the functionality of the code they have already written and for them to analytically detect the bug in their script. The job of a developer, just like any other job, contains many more different tasks that you may currently be unaware of until you dig in deeper. After this point, it becomes questionable whether or not AI can actually take over the full job.

AI can perform tasks relatively quickly and easily based on Internet data, but this does not mean that it can perform the tasks we believe it can perform at the human level or far enough above the human level to benefit handsomely from its returns. Large AI systems take information from the Internet and make inferences based on the information it has gathered. A lot of what we may think about AI from listening to non-technical social media influencers, news outlets, and celebrities are pure exaggerations that are only assumed over the hype that they themselves are spreading and seeing on their social media pages from other non-technical people and news outlets. At the same pace of biased news spreading, there are many wrong views of AI spreading also. We currently live in a very interconnected society that favors news that either creates excitement, laughter, or fear, and out of all these three categories, fear is usually the most prevalent. With too few people knowing about how AI internally works and most experts being unable to explain it in a simple way to the general public, people started fearing about these superintelligent algorithms whether or not they should continue to be developed.

Everything that is new or understudied people would fear the most about, even if they may cause much less destruction. Experiments have gone on to prove this point by showing that even though more deaths occur by bathtubs every single year than by sharks, 99 percent of people would say that a shark causes more fatalities because much less is known about sharks than bathtubs. AI is currently being viewed from a very similar perspective. The personal computer, which has already automated many jobs, is today perceived as something which is actually an enhancement to labor.

After the coronavirus pandemic was over, people began looking for the next big sensational story, and AI just happened to come into the picture. ChatGPT-3 was released in December last year and started making major headlines after Microsoft made a $10,000,000,000 investment into it. The sudden news about AI from everywhere at once has pushed many people to believe this is as big of a deal as the 2020 presidential election or the COVID-19 pandemic. This ignited a lot of bias and false theories about the subject, just as the other events have, but on a much larger scale. This whirlwind of events surrounding the advent of AI has sparked people to wonder about and become afraid of something they know barely anything about.

AI still has so much untapped positive potential in the world if it is continued to be developed for many tasks, such as aiding humans in creating breakthrough innovations in healthcare that can allow people around the world to live forever or providing advice on how to save the earth from an incoming mega-sized asteroid. The possibilities are endless, but for us to continue developing AI, we will need more people to realize how AI works and educate them on why they should not be very afraid of it. After all, in case something ever does go wrong with AI, the more people know about it, the more quickly action can be taken to stop a catastrophe from occurring. If people can learn to be allies with AI instead of enemies, people can make a lot of improvements with their own lifestyles for the better, and we can continue making big leaps in solving some of the world's biggest problems.

So how can we change our perspective about AI? Well, as the experiments with the question of the shark and the bathtub prove, people need to learn more about the internal workings of AI to see that it is not a destructive, black box force that humans should fear, but a very intelligently designed network of algorithms that work together to produce results to complex problems.

The reason why AI is called artificial intelligence to begin with anyways is the fact that it was modeled after our own brains. The algorithms are actually designed in a way to be very similar to the way our own brain processes information for images, sound, and text. So there isn't too much to fear but rather to learn. In this book, *Rethinking AI*, we will learn about how AI internally works, beginning from the most basic algorithms to algorithms that directly replicate the functions of the brain and are part of some of today's largest which are used in some for the most famous AI algorithms such as Midjourney, an algorithm for generating beautiful artfully made images, and Google's Bard AI, a highly intelligent text generation algorithm. Through learning about these algorithms, you can keep this question in your head about whether or not AI should be feared as much as it is in today's news, and you can make the decision for yourself. Of course, if anything is used in the wrong way, it can become dangerous, but this does not mean that today's AI can immediately fall into the wrong hands.

To begin learning about AI though, we cannot look at today's ultra-complex algorithms, such as ChatGPT, right out of the box and peek through the millions of lines of code at individual parts without knowing the intuition behind how the algorithms actually work. The intuition explaining AI has, for a long time, stayed in the world of academia due to its complexities in the use of higher-level mathematics, including multivariate calculus with a combination of complex statistics to explain how it works. But we don't need the most explicit tools in mathematics to know how something at the most basic level works. By using simple mathematics to explain concepts and imagine concepts that were once explained by tens of whiteboards of long calculations in a lecture hall.

We will also begin at the point in time when AI was created to get a glimpse of what it looked like before and what process it took to get to where it is now. Knowing all this will enable you to know why AI has even been made in the first place and where it has been made. You will also learn why a device such as ChatGPT did not exist back during the time when Apple was founded. So let's begin our adventure in the world of AI by taking a trip back to the 1950s, a time when technology was much more simple yet also much more complicated!

Where Did It All Begin?

AI today can create just about anything digital that comes to mind, such as writing an algorithm for an entire app to creating a picture so beautiful it can fool a human into thinking the artwork was created by another human. But AI wasn't always this powerful; it started as only a technique to differentiate between pictures of cats and dogs. The first AI system was created in 1951 by Christopher Strachey, a British computer scientist at the University of Oxford. The AI system was used for attempting to beat humans in a game of checkers. This checkers-playing system was not at all comparable to the current systems we have today, but for 1951, a time about fifteen years before the personal computer was developed, it was a substantial achievement.

A few notable other innovations in AI around this time include the perceptron created by Frank Rosenblatt, one of the first AI algorithms and a key algorithm that was used as the building block for many modern-day algorithms which was used for recognizing cats and dogs from each other. LISP, created by John McCarthy, is a programming language still used today specifically made for creating AI applications, and the term *artificial intelligence* originated from a research paper submitted in 1955 at Dartmouth University. These innovations kickstarted the field of AI and established its connection with computing. Notable ideas of AI have existed as early as 1308, such as *Ars generalis ultima* (the Ultimate General Art), published by Ramon Llull, but until the 1950s, people did not have the computing resources and technology to integrate applications of artificial intelligence with computers.

Even in the 1950s, AI development was still very slow because of the slower technologies used inside computers. This led to a period of time known as the AI winter, which lasted from 1974 to

1993. During this period, funding dried up for AI projects and little progress was being made in the field. In 1993, new technologies released by Intel filled in the computational power gap and ended the winter along with jumpstarting growth in the field continued at a much more accelerated pace than ever before. With all kinds of new powerful devices and the Internet available to share new ideas and thoughts, researchers from all around the world had the tools to create brand new models based on Frank Rosenblatt's perceptron algorithm to create more advanced AI algorithms such as those used in language translation and image generation.

New algorithms based on probability calculations and linear algebra have also emerged during this time that are primarily used for predicting a binary outcome, such as true or false, and others for predicting the probability of an event from 0 to 1.0. These algorithms have become the basis for more complex models such as Google's LAMBDA algorithm (an early generative AI model from Google), ChatGPT, and Google's Bard.

The history of AI can be astounding to visualize, how within sixty years AI has made very big leaps, going from an idea by philosophers to becoming a mainstream technology with the invention of the computer, which made it accessible to everyone. But why has it taken such a long time for a technology specifically like ChatGPT to emerge given the long history of AI? How did AI go from recognizing pictures of cats and dogs to creating a picture to mimic Claude Monet? How is it possible for AI to evolve this quickly from something very simple into such a powerful algorithm?

There are two components: the first is the computational power behind AI, and the second is the algorithmic power behind AI. We will first focus on the computational power behind AI since the algorithmic power of AI would be nonexistent without the computational power. The computational power is responsible for the execution of the algorithm. What good is having an algorithm on paper for the next Google Bard if your computer will take 1,500 years to execute the program? One of the main reasons why ChatGPT had to be released in November of 2022 is the computational power available during that time. Advanced chips such as the Ryzen 7000 advanced microdevices processor or the Intel Core i7 processor have made it possible for developers to test ChatGPT out in the first place.

RAM, CPU, and Bits

To run an AI model on any device, all the computations associated with doing operations to process data given as input to an AI model have to be processed by the RAM (random access memory) of the device and to perform other computations associated with short-term memory. Think about the data being processed through the RAM like a simple piece of data to be stored in memory that will need to be accessed very quickly, very soon. This can be the equivalent of prefrontal cortex in your brain, where your mind can store a memory of where you placed your phone inside your house.

The RAM of the computer aids in performing processes such as booting it up and running applications with high-intensity computations required for runtime, including games, some modeling software, and running AI models. RAM allows the computer to access pieces of data in the form of integers within the computer that are represented as electrical currents throughout the device. These numerical pieces of data stored in the RAM allow the computer to represent anything from a regular number to the color of a hat on an avatar. In terms of machine learning, these are just regular numbers and also signs for operations.

The RAM stores data, but what good is storing data when you cannot do anything with it? This is where the CPU comes into play. The CPU (central processing unit) is the part of the computer which performs all of the mathematical operations: addition, subtraction, multiplication, and division. All computational programs, no matter how simple, require mathematical operations to be performed between pieces of data to be executed.

Think about the window of a simple application with just some basic text in the center saying "Hello, world." The position of the piece of text can be represented as a coordinate of how far up from the bottom of the window and how far from the left of the window the text is, such as one inch up from the bottom of the screen and one inch from the left. The computer is doing calculations to find out where on the screen to display the text. If I want the text of an application I am running to be centered in the middle of the screen when I resize the window, the computer will need to change the coordinates of the piece of text depending on where the new middle of the window is. This would be half of the width of the application window's height and half of its width.

What about the color of the text? The color of the text is represented as an RGB value, a color value of red, blue, and green tints. These tints can be represented as numerical values from 0 to 255. If I want the text to change when I click on it from being blue to being green, I need to subtract 255 from the blue value and add 255 to the green value. As you are beginning to see, very simple operations within the computer require the use of unique mathematical operations to be processed since all data inside the computer is represented in numerical form, primarily patterns of 1s and 0s or binary values, to create a simple piece of information. A 1 at the most basic level indicates an electrical current, and a 0 indicates no current. Patterns like these can be used to form integers, such as 2 with two positive electrical currents, and for odd numbers like 3, two currents of electricity and one current of an absence of electricity. With this method to represent integers, you can also represent words of any form.

Binary Numbers

In binary, a number is represented as a pattern of 1s and 0s so it can be processed as a series of electrical pulses by the CPU and RAM. The binary number system includes only two numbers, 1 and 0, and every single unique digit within the regular number system needs to be represented by them. The digits in a binary number are represented as a placeholder for a number of 2 to the power of the place of the digit in the binary number. For example, in the binary number 110, the first number from the right represents 2 to the power of 1, the 1 in the number after the zero to the right represents 2 to the power of 2, and the number to the right of it represents 2 to the power of 4. In binary, numbers are read from right to left, and each of the values of the digits divided by two are tallied up if the number in its place is 1. If there is a 0 in a digit's place, then the value of a digit in the place is not accounted for in the total value of the binary number. Similarly to how there can be only two states in a transistor (the core building block of the computer found in all processors for representing binary values): the on or the off state.

Using this logic, a longer number like 34,432 can be represented in binary by 1000011010000000. The first one in the number represents the value of 2 to the power of 8, which is 256 since the number is in the eighth position or eight spots from the right. The second 1 in the number is ten spots to the right and represents the number 1024. The third 1 in the number is eleven spots from the right and represents the number 2048. The fourth 1 in the number is the last digit sixteen spots from the right, which represents the number 65,536. Together, when each of these numbers is divided by two and added, the result is the original number in the base ten or decimal system of 34,432.

Inside the computer, in a transistor, the on state indicates a pulse of electricity flowing through the transistor, and the latter condition represents an off state. This is why binary numbers were made to be used for representing information inside computers. Most modern computers can process up to 64-bit and 32-bit numbers. This would mean that the highest number that can be stored on a 64-bit computer would be 0111111111111111111111111111111111111111 11111111111111111111111111111, a number which contains sixty-three ones and one zero at the end. The numbers of 1s and 0s are called bits in computer science.

This method is also used to encode numbers that represent letters that make up words. The ASCII language (American Standard Code for information exchange) is a method of representing upper- and lowercase letters with unique digits that was created by Bob Bemer, a computer scientist at IBM, in 1961 for a universal way to represent information inside computers. Lowercase letters have values from 97 to 122, and all uppercase letters have values from 65 to 90. Even simple operations like hitting backspace on your keyboard or escape also have their own ASCII codes to have the computation processed by the computer's operating system and to represent the output on the screen. The ASCII code for backspace is 08, and the ASCII code for escape is 27. These are examples of pieces of data that the computer can run mathematical operations on within the CPU to modify the output of.

If everything within the computer is represented within a numerical form, imagine how many operations the computer has to run each second for a program like Microsoft Excel. Can the CPU keep up with this demand of use for our modern-day programs? Very well, actually! The average CPU can process 1,800,000,000 operations a second! The most demanding software where CPU matters a lot for performance are video games due to the high-definition graphics and character motion.

But what about a basic AI program? Surely, you would think that a basic application to recognize a cat from a dog would require less operations to be performed than when using a complex program such as Excel. It definitely does not have as heavy a load as Excel with not needing to perform mathematical operations using a spreadsheet that require geometry to resize, select, and mathematical calculations that you order the computer to do when you type simple commands into the program to process inputs in the spreadsheet in a certain way, but this doesn't mean it is a computationally light process either.

To start, the computer is required to perform thousands of computations on the RGB values of each of the pixels of the image to learn to distinguish which patterns of them make up a picture that looks to humans as a cat and the same for dogs and which don't make an image of a cat or a dog at all, and it cannot do this by simply looking at the image we would as humans. The computer can only process information in binary so the information needs to be broken down to contain as little abstraction (simplification) for it to be able to be turned into this form. Then the algorithm needs to actually make the mathematical predictions (which we will learn about later) on the new representation of the image about whether or not it contains a cat or a dog. All these steps require computation that need to be performed on every single pixel in the image which can grow very fast depending on the type of image and the quality of it.

There is no modern-day application that is void of needing many computational processes to run it. If Google had launched in 1980, it would not be as successful as it is today. In 1980, the only processors available were the Intel 8086 and Intel 386. These processors were 16-bit (able to handle integers up to 16 bits, or in other words up to 1111111111111111 in binary and 65,536 in computational processes) and have been able to perform 0.33 to one million operations per second on average, a far cry from the 1.8 billion operations our current CPUs can process.

In addition to needing to process current information and store it, the data also needs to be displayed on the screen somehow, and this, as you know by now, also requires math. This is the job of the GPU (graphics processing unit); it is used for determining how to display the data on the screen of your device. Imagine you have told ChatGPT to draw a basic square that you would like to be two inches high and two inches wide, that is blue, and in the center. How would ChatGPT go about rendering or placing the image it generates on the screen? The GPU would start by determining how many pixels on the screen are equal to two inches and also send information to the pixels on your screen about what color they should be. In addition, if you would like your square to be filled, the GPU would square the number of pixels that are equal to two inches on the screen to find out how many pixels would take up the size of the inside of the square. Since you have also told ChatGPT to draw the square in the middle of the screen, the GPU will target the pixels in the middle of the screen to modify them to appear in the way that we described.

The GPU connects to the CPU to receive data that has recently been processed to display on screen. To be able to do all these things, the GPU itself does not have the data it needs to perform computations to begin with. It is made up of many parts, such as a processor, similar to that in the CPU, to do the computations regarding the dimensions of the shapes and the mathematics behind figuring out which pixels to connect to for displaying the shape.

Accompanied by this processor is the VRAM (video random access memory), which, as the name suggests, is another storage chip for short-term memory, but this time for the memory that came from the CPU and the data to send to the pixels on the monitor (the screen of the device) that is currently being modified by the processor in the GPU. Lastly, to be able to display this information on the screen, the GPU needs to connect somehow to the monitor of the device. This is done through a tiny cable within the inside of the device to create the image on the screen. All of this work is done just to create a simple blue two-inch-by-two-inch rectangle on the screen!

You may now be asking yourself, what does the GPU have to do with AI? If the GPU is a component of your device for rendering graphics, how does it help your computer to run an AI algorithm? Well, the GPU is a processing unit similar to the CPU, and while it does have an additional purpose, it is still used for performing operations with data that comes directly from the CPU. In some cases, if the CPU has a very heavy load of data that you would like to process using your AI algorithm, this can put a large strain on the CPU to process it alone.

While processors are getting more advanced by the year, the amount of data that needs to be run through them for computations is also growing as developers keep developing more advanced applications for more efficient and intelligent purposes. In cases such as these, using the CPU alone can sometimes take hours or days to process very large sets of data you may run through an AI algorithm. During these hours or days of waiting for your computer to process the data, the computer will also become unbelievably slow due to all of its computational power being allocated to your CPU processing the data through your AI algorithm, and you won't even be able to use your device for just about anything else while waiting.

This is why developers have created the ability to allocate parts of the data being processed by your AI algorithm to your GPU to be processed. The GPU being used for processing the data can bring down the time constraint for finishing running your AI algorithm for down by quite a lot, sometimes by up to nineteen times compared to when using the CPU alone.

Unfortunately, GPUs are not found in every device, specifically older devices, but all devices have a system for rendering graphics on the screen. GPUs can either be built into the device or they could be a card that can be placed inside the computer of the device, so many machine learning engineers (software engineers specializing in AI algorithms) are doing this to save money from needing to purchase a device with a built-in GPU.

We now know that CPUs, RAM, and GPUs are the main components to process the data that runs through an AI algorithm, but how do they all interact? Well, the RAM needs to be connected to the CPU to process the data which may be allocated to it from the CPU. The CPU, to be able to display the data on the screen, needs to be connected to the GPU. All these components are connected together through a motherboard. The motherboard is the main circuit of the device which allows all of the components of the computer to communicate with each other. Everything from the USB stick of your mouse to the speakers of your computer is connected to it. The motherboard allows all components to send bits to each other using a pin grid array. The pin grid array is a set of pins that keep the components attached to the motherboard and allow them to accept the pulses of electricity that get sent through them through the motherboard, representing the bits of data the device is operating with. Changing the functionality of components on the motherboard can change the way that the device functions.

Modern-day motherboards are also the reason why we can run the same kind of software made for Windows on all Windows devices. This is one of the reasons why you need to choose the operating system you are using when downloading software. In the past, many computers, such as IBM PCs, have used a motherboard that was specifically configured to run only software made for their kinds of devices. This annoyed many users who had to specifically look for software tailored to that kind of device, which led to a team experimenting with reassembling the parts on the motherboards in the IBM PCs to create new devices to run any kind of software. The team that did this created a business out of creating these different devices with innovative motherboards called Compaq.

So far, we have gone over CPUs, RAM, and GPUs. All these components together are what allow the computer to process data for AI algorithms, but what about other parts? Well, modern-day computers require many more components than just these three to function, but for the purpose of understanding AI algorithms, you only need to understand how these three components work. The computer primarily uses these components for doing the computations that give us results from the algorithms.

Defining a Computer

A computer is defined as a device to perform computations with using bits of data. In the past, there even used to be specific jobs for human mathematicians to perform this process. Computers are nothing more than just giant very powerful calculators that have been continuously innovated on over to be able to be used for many more things than just adding up numbers, so computers without programs are like calculators without equations to execute—they are bulky devices which need a query (a prompt to give to the device such as an equation in a calculator) to actually experience their power and usefulness.

For most of history, computers were used in mainly scientific and cooperate settings for processing data related to research, tedious mathematical operations and processing business data. Computers also were usually the sizes of rooms and had to be reprogrammed every single time they had to do new computations. This can be a reason to why for a long time throughout history, there hasn't been too much innovation done with these technologies, and there wasn't any thought that has crossed people's minds about a computer being used for tasks other than academic and business purposes until the 1970s with the release of a personal computer DIY kit called the Altair, which sparked the creation of Microsoft Windows and Apple's Mac OS. Most advances in computing were created throughout history for the reason of military purposes, such as the Second world War which created an incentive for very notable innovations in computing that still stay with us today.

Computers are a device that we can use our imaginations with to create just about anything we would like with. Even if you are not a programmer, you still can create amazing videos on Adobe Premiere

Pro or amazing designs on Canva. Computers are one of the most revolutionary inventions in the history of mankind that doesn't have a single creator. Many innovators throughout history, such as Charles Babbage, Robert Noyce, Grace Hopper, and Alan Turing, each contributed a small piece of work to the field of computing which has been added up over time to create our smartphones that we have today. There has been no single person to patent the computer. These increments of work have also led us to today's advanced AI technologies used in systems such as ChatGPT and Google's Bard AI within the field of artificial intelligence. AI will shine a new light on what computers can do and what we can do with them, which is very important in an increasingly complex world. AI, using the computer's processing power through the CPU, GPU, and RAM, can help us to understand some of the most complex systems out there and maybe even provide us with advice on how to solve some of societies' biggest problems to today.

Operating systems were the first way we opened up interaction to these powerful machines, and AI is the next big step. AI can communicate with you in a way that a human can such as in the models of ChatGPT and Bard AI. They serve to be the next frontier for filling our knowledge gaps and having companions that can be as intelligent if not more intelligent than us. We have a superpower with this creation for being able to do things that we never thought we could to being able to do many with AI, but to be able to use something right, you need to know first how does it work. Knowing how something works will allow you to be able to see it from a new angle, an angle in which you can come up with great ideas on how to use it in, and ways in which you may even be able to advance it.

While it might seem daunting to think about how something such as ChatGPT works, from the beginning, as you continue learning about AI, a map in your mind will form for how everything works. All knowledge in a subject like artificial intelligence can be thought of as a map of different concepts you learn leading to newer concepts such as paths on a physical map leading to new corners which when you turn in can lead to newer paths, and if you follow all of the paths correctly on the map it can lead you to your desired destination.

Computers have been around since the 1800s, but they were not the kind of devices you would see today on shelves. Computers were giant and had to constantly be reprogrammed for every single new program they were given to execute. We are lucky to live in a time when doing almost any computational task with the average computer is possible, so it's a great time to be learning about a technology that we can use with them that is changing the world rapidly, and how you can use it to your benefit in your everyday life, innovate with it, and know how AI models can be made to be more inclusive and safe. So let's begin!

The Inside of AI

The definition of AI that we have described recently, as an algorithm learning from loads of data, is a very broad explanation. What kind of algorithm is AI made up of? How many are there? What makes each algorithm unique? How do they connect with each other? The data also can pose questions, such as what is the data that AI algorithms use? Where do we get the data from? How much data do we need?

These questions are no accident for anyone who has never received formal education on what AI is and how they can create it on their own. In some cases, AI, even to some of the most educated experts within the field, can sometimes seem like a daunting black box (an object in which you are not sure of how it fully functions and is created). With models becoming very advanced and large, their functionality can start to operate with as much unpredictability as the global economy does. In other terms, large AI models have been created to have so much processing ability of data that they can be thought of as having the complexity of the stock market. It is another very complex system which comprises of moving gears which are buyers and sellers and methods that they use such as short selling that are going on all at the same time (within one day when the stock exchange is open within any country). They sometimes conflict with each other, leading to a bumpy trend line you would see on the graph of the price of a certain stock. Sometimes the conflicts between buyers and sellers can also be in short trends, leading to large spikes and falls within the stock price equating a spikey line.

In large and complex AI models, there can be a similar relationship as in the stock market between the parts of the AI algorithm. There can be many parts of the algorithm producing conflicting pieces of data and results to each other and parts of the algorithm that are meant to make sense of these conflicting results, and data similar to how the trader or investor in the stock market is meant to make sense of all the conflicting changes, such as between the puts and the calls of different stocks, the movement of the interest rate, company news, and the movement of the overall market. Modern AI algorithms are designed to be powerful to the point where they sometimes edge beyond our understanding of how they fully work, scaring many people away from learning the discipline. But unless you want to become a researcher working on developing the Midjourney model or DALL-E model at OpenAI, you will rarely encounter such AI models that function as unpredictably as the stock market does. Most AI models, while still containing conflicting results in order for them to properly produce results are understandable with proper analysis. Everything has basic building blocks that when you understand you can understand the entirety of the structure that they build. The line blurs only between the parts, and the structure becomes so massive and detailed, such as Bard AI or Midjourney. Basic AI algorithms are much easier to learn than you may think right now.

AI algorithms were created to model the human brain and the way that children learn. Children learn through their brains receiving input, their brains processing this input and generating thoughts from it that it turns into actions which can be either physical or mental from these thoughts. One key part of this process is that the more an action is repeated, the more intricate and rational the thought generated by the input data becomes, allowing children over time to get better at doing certain things such as walking and talking and more complex processes such as playing soccer.

Researchers have designed AI algorithms to replicate this method in the way that they need to be retrained to make better assumptions about certain types of data, such as identifying whether a picture contains a cat or a dog. Just like the process of learning for children, AI algorithms also have steps they take to be trained, including inputting the data, preprocessing the data, using the mathematical algorithm that draws insights from the data, and receiving the results from the model to evaluate and then modify the algorithm or the results accordingly. In addition, computer science has given us the unique advantage of visualization tools that people can use to assess the accuracy of these models and visualize the results in a clean and precise format.

The First Piece

The first building block of AI is the data itself, as it is required for every single AI algorithm. For any learning system, such as our own brains, to work, we need to have a way of interacting with the world. This in our own bodies is our five senses: our hearing, smell, touch, vision, and taste. This data we perceive by pulses within our brain, that later lead us to create conclusions about it. Touching a hot stove will generate data felt in your brain as an unpleasant reaction in the form of painwhich will give you an indication to not touch the hot stove again.

Just like the data that humans can collect through their different senses, the data within AI models can be either text or numerical but will need to be processed into numerical data when the model is trained on for simplification purposes and further processed to be standardized to reduce the error that may be attached to numerical data that is over too big a range. Data which is not converted to numerical form in one way or another will not be able to be processed by the algorithms since they rely on mathematical operations to make logical conclusions on the data. In the field of artificial intelligence, this step is called preprocessing.

Going back to the analogy of the brain of a child, if the child is receiving too much input at the same time, there is a chance that they can become distracted from what actually matters, and they might make a wrong assumption about the input they received about a certain action, so all data whether textual or numerical that will be processed through an AI model needs to be reduced to as small of a range as possible to reduce the risk of an incorrect assumption. To do this with numerical data, first outliers need to be removed and then the data needs to be scaled to be within a certain range of values.

The two most commonly used methods to do this are standardization which will reduce your values to being in a range between the same small positive and negative numbers, such as –4 and 4. The second methos is normalization, a method that will reduce all the values in your dataset to being within a range of 0 to 1. Standardization is used when there are multiple different types of features in data that need to go through the AI model. The range will correlate with the amount of different features present in the data. For example, the range –4 to 4 would be best used if the data has four different features. The number of features is equivalent to the number of unique values in your numerical data or values that are different from others.

An example of this would be a dataset that has ten numbers: [902, 347, 781, 347, 902, 902, 781, 347, 781, 902]. This dataset has three different categories since there are three different types of values in this set: 902, 347, and 781. To standardize a single value of the data, you would subtract the average of the data from the current data point. The value would then be divided by the sum of each value in the data subtracted by the average and then divided by the previous value in the data. (If you did not fully understand the process in the last sentence, feel free to read over it again. This process in particular requires many different steps that might be difficult to understand without thinking a little about it first). Normalization, on the other hand, is used when the data has only two different values which can be encoded into 1 or 0, allowing for very easy distinction and processing of the data. Normalization is done by taking the current value you would like to normalize in your dataset and subtracting it from the minimum value of the data. This result would then be divided by the difference of the maximum and the minimum of the dataset. This operation would be performed on each of the values in the data to normalize the entire set.

Data we use our model with will need to be split up into four different categories, such as the data we use for the independent variable which includes the data that the model takes as the input (the first data the model learns from to familiarize itself with the data or the core data of the set), data for the independent variable (data that is used to validate how well the model has learnt from the training data), data in training which we use for teaching the model the patterns of the data with, and data in testing set which we use for comparing the performance of the model with to the data in the training set. The amount of data that would be allocated for the testing of the AI model is always less than the amount of data used to train the model with since the model to learn patterns from the data more carefully it will require more data for the task. Generally the amount of data that is allocated for training is 80 percent of the total set.

We have learned about how numerical data can be processed into a smaller range, but what would we do about textual data? Does textual data get processed the same way? Not exactly. We have learned about ASCII, which is the standardized method worldwide for mapping letters in text to numbers that can later be turned into binary, but texts do not get mapped to the exact same numbers from ASCII since the range of values is huge. Also, characters such as full stops (.), commas (,), and ampersands (&) should be removed to reduce distractions in the data. In a similar way to how a dataset full of data that is too different from each other can give the AI model distractions, potentially leading it to producing the wrong result, basic characters in text and sentences that are two long also have the ability of doing this too. Luckily there are many methods available of helping us do this that have been created, including stemming, lemmatization, tokenization, removing punctuation and removing stop words.

Removing commas, full stops, and ampersands is part of the method of removing punctuation. Punctuation, within the context of an AI algorithm, does not really mean too much for the processing of the data. Computers can only deal with numbers at the level they operate, and they cannot do any tasks unless you indicate what they are supposed to do. Computers cannot read a sentence for understanding unless you use an AI algorithm for the computer to grab insights from a sentence processed in a format that the computer can understand for it to be able to give you a result. At the most basic level, it is not the computer that is actually learning anything from the data; it is the algorithm that is learning from the input. The computer is just executing (running) the algorithm.

In this context, if shortening up the sentence will not make the sentence much easier AI model, why not continuing to remove distraction from the sentence by getting rid of some words that don't add meaning? These words, referred to as stop words, do not have a logical relation to the sentence, such as *is, actually, a, be,* and *at.* These words are simply padded into the sentence for the purpose of adding more context and making it easier to understand for humans, but for computers, this will stand in the way of our algorithm being able to interpret the sentence accuracy. For example in the sentence, "The king has been crowned," the meaning of the sentence is only portrayed in a few words. *Been* for example relates only to support the context of the sentence such as the fact that the king was crowned in the past, but it doesn't relate to the overall interpretation of the sentence, and the *-ed* at the end of the word *crown* can already give you a good enough indication that the sentence was written in the past tense.

If you are reading this sentence for the context, you would just interpret the meaning from the words *king* and *crowned* not *has, been,* and *the.* Therefore by removing the stop words, you can keep the meaning within the sentence and also shorten it up to a great extent. In the example, we have removed three out of the five words in the sentence by removing all of the words that do not contribute to the original meaning of the sentence.

This method, though, is not always used. The removal of stop words can sometimes have a negative impact the accuracy of the model, such as in an AI algorithm for detecting good and bad reviews. Words such as *not* are counted as stop words within the language, and removing them from a sentence in a review can change the sentiment. This is why there are many different ways of shortening sentences to be input into AI algorithms.

Another way of shortening up the amount of textual data to be processed by an AI algorithm is by splitting up sentences by the word. Some parts of sentences include characters that are not punctuation but are still not necessary to interpreting the meaning of the sentence; "I'd like this flavor" is an example. In this sentence, there is an apostrophe between *I* and *d,* indicating the shortened phrase for "I would." This apostrophe in a similar way to punctuation also can create useless data for the AI algorithm to get distracted by. Removing the apostrophe allows us to perform the same change to the sentence as by stemming the words. The main way of an AI algorithm to perform this operation is by splitting up sentences by the words, which automatically would remove any ampersands from shortened up phrases in the sentence. The sentence "I'd like this flavor" can be split up by the words into "I'd like this flavor." This process is called tokenization, removing tokens or pieces of the sentence like the apostrophe to shorten it up.

All these processes that we have mentioned are part of a field of AI called natural language processing (in short NLP), which means what the name suggests. It is about machines (computers) interpreting human language whether it is in English or Mandarin into numerical data which later can be turned into binary data. NLP techniques are used whenever text is required to be processed before being run in an AI algorithm. The field of NLP has its main applications within AI algorithms ranging from large language models (AI algorithms like ChatGPT to Bard AI which can output sophisticated responses comparable to that of humans) to language translators and algorithms to summarize your document. NLP recently has become a very step forward in the field of AI for allowing AI algorithms to be created that can have more human-friendly input (input to the algorithm that is readable easily to humans). NLP is one of the most important advances in the field that is responsible for the creation of our advanced AI models today, so it is worth knowing how it works under the hood to be able to understand them.

We have so far learned about methods of NLP including stemming, lemmatization, tokenization, and removing punctuation and stop words, but what about arranging the data for input to the AI model? Where does the AI algorithm read the data from? The data that the model is trained on comes from a file that is connected to the file of the AI algorithm and has the data arranged in a way for the algorithm to be easily able to read. In different programing languages, different methods are used for reading input from a file, and depending on which language is used, a library (a group of different commands within a programming language to perform certain tasks) is used to read line by line from the file. Files used for data in the field of AI and computing are usually comma-separated files (also called CSV files), which contain the data arranged by rows holding one or many pieces of data in different columns, with each row being numbered. The columns within these files have names that represent certain types of data such as temperature, balance, and score. The name "comma-separated files" comes from the fact that the columns in the files are separated by commas. These files contain data that can be very easily organized into an Excel spreadsheet document but are typed out in pure text. For this reason, there needs to be a clear delimiter (separator) between the columns of data. Columns in this file can be separated in this manner: [column1, column2, column3, column4, column5]. With the addition of a row number before the row, the columns now look like this: [0, column1, column2, column3, column4, column5].

The data can be structured differently depending on what type of learning method you are using for your AI algorithm. There are two types of learning that can be used for an AI algorithm: supervised learning and unsupervised learning.

Supervised learning is a method of an AI algorithm having a correct piece of data for output to compare the output that it generated. For this type of learning to be used, the data must contain a label column, that contains data such as true or false, which is what the AI algorithm should output when running the specific type of data from that row through the model. This data can be processed to enter the AI model in many different ways. Depending whether the data is meant to be of only two different types (e.g., right, wrong), it can be encoded (processed by the computer) into 0s and 1s that the device can directly read. In the field of AI, this is called one-hot encoding. A pattern of 1s and 0s can be used if the number of different items in the labels' column is more than two, such as [bad, good, neutral]. Data in the labels column can also come in the form of probabilities, such as 0.89 or 0.21.

An example of this type of learning can be depicted by teaching a dog how to do a new trick. If the dog does the trick successfully, the dog earns a treat. If the dog doesn't do the trick well, the dog gets no treats. This type of feedback loop allows the dog to realize when do they do the trick well. This allows for the dog to go back to remembering what it did when it did the trick well to doing the trick again when it needs to. The dog getting a treat back for the trick he did well is comparing its performance to what it is supposed to be and the dog earning an award for it, which is positive feedback. This will increase the likelihood for the dog to do the trick correctly again. AI algorithms can be trained in the exact same method as the dog in a type of supervised learning called reinforcement learning.

In unsupervised learning, the AI algorithm simply learns through repetition, gathering new insights from the data and adjusting parts of the algorithm meant to gain certain insights to be different and more suitable for processing a specific type of data. An example of this can be finding your way around a maze. You don't originally know where to go, so you need to try different routes. If the route you are currently on leads to a dead end, you go back and take a different route. Do this over and over again, and eventually, you will find your way out of the maze. In this process, you are teaching yourself how the maze works, just like the AI algorithm is teaching itself how to get the right insights from the data.

This leads us to the next building block of an AI algorithm: the actual algorithm itself. The type of AI algorithm used is based on the type of learning that the AI model is doing with the data, which we have already learned falls within two different categories: supervised and unsupervised. But what about more specific types of learning? Within supervised learning and unsupervised learning, there are specific methods used to build algorithms.

Specific types of learning methods within supervised learning are part of a subset of the field of AI called machine learning. The models used with these types of learning are also called machine learning models instead of AI models specifically. Some of the methods within supervised learning include regression, decision trees, *k*-nearest neighbors, naive Bayes classifiers, classification, and logistic regression. These learning methods are older than unsupervised learning methods since they require less complex algorithms and much less power to execute. However, they are still very useful today and continue to be used in many modern applications that require a large use of historical data.

One of the reasons why supervised learning has fallen out of fashion in our time compared to unsupervised learning algorithms like ChatGPT is due to the dislike of continuous need for historical data to train the algorithm to produce new results. Nevertheless, there are enough applications for these types of models in our modern world, and the endless buzz about the newest technologies available out there all started as something very simple. When the simple, older, less attractive technology is ignored, you will never be able to understand how the modern, quick, and sleek version of the technology works. This is why, to understand AI at the highest level, we need to begin with the most basic algorithm in the field of AI: regression.

How Much More?

Regression is the most basic learning type out of all supervised learning methods. It uses one of the most simple processes of finding patterns in data: linear regression. Linear regression is one of the most basic concepts you need to understand many things in the world work. There are many things in this world that have linear-oriented systems, and linear regression is the method we use to find a pattern in them. Almost anything in the world can represented in numbers which we can turn into data and using it we can find a pattern between them describing what we are observing, such as a cup of water filling up from a faucet.

If the faucet is left alone, it will keep delivering the same amount of water into the cup per second unless there is some kind of intervention, like putting your hand under it or turning up the flow. Linear regression works with two different variables or categories of data. In the case of the cup of water, one of the variables is the amount of water being poured into the cup per second, and the other is the amount of time in seconds. Using this equation, if the amount of water that has been poured into the glass per second is thirty fluid ounces, after sixty seconds, there will be 1,800 fluid ounces of water inside the cup.

In the world of AI, linear regression is a very simple algorithm to understand both the inputs (what is going into the equation) and the output (what is being produced by the equation). This makes it a perfect algorithm to begin with when learning how machine learning models work through learning. Linear regression, like all other machine learning models, is used from a library of commands associated with machine learning in a programming language. Linear regression is first initialized (set up) as a class in the language that can be called upon within the algorithm. A class is a set of variables (commands that hold a value similar to a variable in mathematics) and functions (commands that allow for runnable commands of code inside them that take inputs and return outputs in a similar way to functions in mathematics and do processes with the variables to produce a different output with them) that wrap them up together and allow them to be used whenever the class is called from the library, which would contain a variety of them that can be used for machine learning algorithms.

Using this class, we would then call on (use) a function for taking as input to the class the training data: the x-train data (the training data that is not what we are trying to predict or the first type of training data described) and the y-train data (the labels that we want the machine learning algorithm to predict, or in other words, the validation data). The algorithm will, using this function, be configured (ready) to perform the calculations on each of the lines of the independent (X-variable) data and use a comparison metric to outline how well it is computing the difference between it and the dependent (Y-variable) data. This will be adjusted until the algorithm has made calculations on all the lines of the X-data.

At the runtime of the algorithm, there won't be any notice of the fact that the computer has actually performed the calculations since the CPU executes millions of commands per second. All you will see is the output of the algorithm, which will be an integer showing the accuracy of the algorithm. The accuracy can be explored with different visualization tools for displaying what the data looks like that it holds or advanced measurements you can use for measuring the amount of error the output has produced. Visualization for different algorithms will depend on the calculations used behind the scenes in the algorithm to make predictions with the data.

In our case of linear regression, this would be the simple equation of a line, which would indicate about how the data is probably going to fit in a graph. With the equation of a line being used to linearly scale all the pieces of data, the best method to graph the results of the predictions would be on a simple linear graph with the results shown as dots that fit along a line showing the general trend of the data. The data in this view can be much more easily analyzed by a human for learning the type of connections that the different categories within the algorithm are being measured by, such as what kind of connection they have to each other. One result of the model might be a visual graph showing a trend within the data, and the performance of the model itself can be visualized alongside it.

Evaluating the Performance of AI Models

The performance can be characterized by the error between the validation data values (values in the y set of data) and the predicted values (the x-values). We need to figure what is a simple way to distinguish all values processed by the model for how the well did the machine learning model do to predict the output for. To do this we would need to turn to methods that can calculate the distance between two different values on a graph. One of these such models is called r squared, a measurement that is used to compare the difference between a point and the overall trend on a graph.

r squared is measured by the sum of all the actual values of y minus the predicted values of y, divided by the sum of all the actual values of y minus the mean (or average) value of the y data. The result of this operation is then subtracted from one to get the value of r squared. This answer will give us a number from zero to one, indicating how close the predicted values are to the actual values in the y data. The higher the number, the closer the points are to the data. However, for nonlinear data, this method will not work. In this case, r squared will not provide a proper estimate since the variance (overall distance from the line) is not equal to the sum of the error variance, calculated by the sum of the actual values of y minus the predicted values of y and the total variance of the model. Additionally, the model can factor in bias represented through more categories of x values within the data, which can skew the calculation of r squared to be higher than it would be if those categories weren't there.

The metric of r squared is a great place to begin for learning how to measure the inaccuracies in the output with a very straightforward way of its measuring process, but it has many fallbacks to using it in more diverse sets of data specifically with more categories of data. Many datasets will encounter this issue so is there straightforward metric that can be used with more categories? There is, and the answer might [mean] much more than you would think.

The metric of the mean squared error is a much more popular and widely used metric with many machine learning models compared to r squared. This metric has a tendency to inflate the error associated with differences between predicted values and actual values, allowing you to see differences that might originally not make a large difference in a much clearer light. With this feature, the mean squared error can be a great metric for measuring models that you would like to have the highest possible accuracy with.

The mean squared error is composed of the sum of the differences between subtracting the predicted values from the y values, squaring the difference, and then dividing this value by the amount of all the values in the dataset. The metric will output a value from 0 at the lowest to infinity at the highest. The closer the value of this metric to 0, the less of the difference there is between the actual and predicted values of y, indicating a more accurate model. It seems like the perfect solution for every model, right? But even though this model may sound like it can very well trump r squared with its perfectionist intention, this metric is still not perfect.

For example, the inflation of the mean squared error metric poses will not give values for errors that that are very close to what the actual values are. This can be connected to how the metric bloats the values of errors in the values that the model might predict in the way that is squares them, making them seem a lot larger than they are. The metric is also not usable among datasets with values scaled to different amounts. For example, if we have a dataset with data after preprocessing that looks like [0.90, 0.34, 0.40, 0.56] and another dataset with [0.034, 0.04, 0.09, 0.056], the output of the metric will be very different in these two instances of the data. Even though the differences between the data and the predicted values are not that far apart, the differences in the type of data that this metric can process will make this metric generate a different answer.

In the field of AI, there is no such thing as the perfect algorithm whether it would be for evaluating the computation or performing it itself. When evaluating a possible solution to a computational problem in the field of AI, it is important to think about what would work best. There is no one-size-fits-all answer. In the case of AI algorithm evaluation metrics, there is always a tradeoff between perfection and scalability. In the case of the mean squared error, only datasets that are entirely standardized can be used. However, it has great capabilities which can allow us to model its use on the next model which builds on top of linear regression: multivariate linear regression.

Multivariate linear regression is as simple as a model that has the exact same functionality as linear regression but can be used with multiple different categories in the dataset representing different groupings of pieces of data that our model can make the assumption from. The name multivariate comes from the words multi- and variable chained together to create a word to describe a type of mathematical discipline that is used whenever there are types of calculations that need to be performed with many different types of variables involved. Basic linear regression uses two different variables, the X- and Y-variables, for training and running our model with one column each. However, with multivariate linear regression, the X-variable encompasses many different categories of values or many different columns within the comma-separated file (CSV file).

The equation for multivariate regression is just like the equation of the line but repeated for every extra category within the data. For example, if there are five different categories within the X-variable inside the data, the equation would, instead of being $y = mx + b$, add an extra $(x + b)$ to the equation four times. The equation after this would become $y = b + mx + mx + mx + mx + mx$ to account for every single extra category in our X-variable.

Multivariate linear regression is trained in the exact same way as the regular linear regression model is, only its input is processed to be in a different way. Since the categories are part of our X-values, we still have only two different values to run the model with, but the different columns within the X-variable need to be selected. Before data preprocessing and the data is split into the X- and Y-variables, the different categories of the dataset need to be selected to be part of the X-variable. The model can work for a dataset with any amount of categories with data that is linear.

The output of this model the same of the output of the regular linear regression model, but with only many more values, since each category is required to have the same amount of values as each other in order to be able to be processed by the machine learning model. Data that is removed for various reasons, including outliers, incorrect values, or null need to be replaced with something else in the dataset.

In a similar way to the linear regression output, it is possible to graph the outputs of this model, but this would require multiple dimensions to graph it. Each category can be thought of as a dimension that is added to the dataset since it is making its own measurement of a type of data in the dataset and it needs its own label. Knowing this graphing, the result might not give you a clear picture of the relationship between the data in the graph, and it is better to avoid. So is there another algorithm that is has visualizable solution?

Another model that is heavily used for regression in machine learning is called a decision tree. A decision tree predicts the characteristics of a new data point based on previous inputs of values into the model, similar to a flowchart. A flowchart is a diagram that shows a process of continuing events in a certain direction connected by arrows. They include cards with text to describe the events and the connection of cards in lower ranks of the diagram to the top card to describe the direction of the events from the first piece of data to the last. Flowcharts allow for great representation of situations that involve a single event (in this case, an attribute of a piece of data) changing the direction of future events.

An example of this can be a flowchart showing whether you are a baby boomer, Gen X, millennial, or Gen Z. For this flowchart, we can use age as the determining characteristic for each of these events. A card at the top can state that you are less than eighty years old since people who are over the age of seventy-nine today are part of a generation called the silent generation that will not be included in our example for simplicity. The direction from the top card of the tree would split out to two cards right below it, asking if you are currently fifty years old or older, and there would be two lines that would branch out from this card depending on how you would answer this question. If you are fifty years old or older, the next card that you would read will ask if you were born before 1980. If you answered no to the question of whether you were older than fifty years old, your next card would be to the left of the card for those who answered no. This card would ask whether you are currently twenty-seven years old or older. Going back to the side of the tree for those who answered that they were over the age of forty-eight, the next question would ask if they are over the age of fifty-nine. For those who answered yes to this question, they would receive the result of baby boomers for their generation. Alternatively, those who answered no to this question would receive the conclusion that they are part of Gen X. On the right side of the tree, if you had answered no to the question of whether you were twenty-seven years old or older, your conclusion would be that you are part of Gen Z, and for those who answered yes, their conclusion would be that they are a millennial.

Decision trees work in a very similar way to this process. At the top of the decision tree is the data point to base all decisions about other data points on for the future which is randomly selected from the dataset. The data point would include a data point with multiple different characteristics of the value, such as categories that this data point fits into from the dataset. There would underneath by a question presented about the top data point, such as whether the value of the new data point is greater than 10, which can be the value of the top data point. If this is true, the next decision will be set to the right card underneath it; if not, the next question will be to the left side. Now you can begin to see where the name decision tree comes from. This model gets its name from its structure imitating a tree in the way that each decision branching out into multiple directions.

In our example, when we have a data point that agrees or disagrees with the given question, this data point would become the next target for new questions to be asked from and conclusions that would determine where to place new points. This process is done for all points in the dataset creating a decision tree with an unimaginable size to look at. Decision trees can even become more complex if there are more options for whether a question is answered in a certain way. In our example, what if instead of asking about whether the next data point has a value that is greater than the value of the point at the top of the tree, there might be a different group we would like for pieces of data that have the same value as the top point to join? This would then require a third direction for the tree to span out into from the top point.

Decision trees can also be used for machine learning methods other than regression by changing the types of decisions made about the data. If we target whether a feature is the same as or different from another data point, we can group it in a certain way. In this way, we can perform classification analysis on points in a dataset by asking questions about the similarity of the features of the points instead of their values for certain features.

Decision trees can easily be mapped onto a graph, in the situation of decision trees used for regression. On this graph, the trend can be easily seen in a staircase like shape. This sudden spikes in the graph creating the staircase structure account for the difference in the value in each next point after a decision has been made on the tree. Of course, the graph still needs to follow a pattern of regression for this use of the tree, and the staircase indeed shows this with its incremental steps upward. In decision trees, you can easily see the connections between the data with its points marked onto the graph and the difference in their values changing the direction of the trend curve to create the staircase shape. A visual interpretation of data is only best when the relationship between the data can actually be clearly seen in a graph, which with all models is not always true.

Graphing the output of the model is only necessary if you are trying to learn the relationship between the different data points, the image they create, and how it can answer your question about why you are performing the analysis on the data points. If there is nothing you can gain from getting a graphical image of the data, it is better to measure the performance of the model and see how accurate your results are through accuracy metrics such as mean squared error, rather than looking at a complex graph that might not give you the answer you want.

If you have just made a model for use by customers, then its performance is what you are looking for, and the data does not need to be visualized. The mean squared error can be applied to this model in the same way as with normal linear regression. Simply provide the X-variable and Y-variable as inputs to the metric and then run the code.

For evaluating this model, the mean squared error in this case might not be very good though for an accurate measurement due to its inaccurate measures, but we still need to use a metric that is compatible with multiple categories to get an accurate estimate. So what should we use? Well, there are other metrics that use a similar method of calculation as the mean squared error but have some differences, such as removing the squaring of the difference between the y-prediction and the actual y-value or removing some of the inflation of the final value of the metric outputs by using a square root.

There are two notable metrics in machine learning for doing this: mean absolute error and root mean squared error. These methods share the characteristic of the summation of the differences between the predicted value of y and the actual value of y and dividing the result by N, giving their name the *mean* part, but also include methods to avoid the problems the mean squared error metric has.

The mean absolute error is the first metric in this category and has the most significant result when measuring the accuracy of a model's results. This metric contains the same calculation as the mean squared error but with the difference of taking the absolute value of the difference between the predicted y-value and the actual y-value. The sum of all the absolute value differences between the predicted y-value and the actual y-value is then multiplied by the number of values in the dataset. This value is then divided by 1 to result in a number from 0 to 1, describing the accuracy of the predicted values of the model.

With an answer within a smaller range and a more precise measurement, this strategy serves as a great substitute for the mean squared error. In a similar way, the root mean squared error, which is usually a good alternative to the mean absolute error, does almost the exact same thing but with the difference of the error results increasing in a linear way. This means that if an error is received for a model that is 20, and another model is scored at 10 using this metric, the model that has scored 20 is two times worse than the model that has scored 10. This can be a straightforward way to compare the accuracy of one model to the other.

Another one of its pros is minimizing the variance in a dataset or the difference between data points and the overall trendline of the data. When the variance is minimized, it results in smaller errors between outliers and the trendline, similar to how normalizing the data during preprocessing minimizes the overall scale of the data, making it less likely to guide the machine learning model to produce an error-prone prediction.

Minimizing the difference between outliers and the overall trendline might not always be a good method for producing more accurate results, though. It should still be noted that outliers can sometimes have significance in a dataset. Depending on the question you are trying to answer with your insights gathered from the model, outliers can sometimes play an important role in validating or challenging the question or assumption.

For example, when running a machine learning model on a dataset measuring the wealth of countries, if we have a dataset about all countries on the planet and different characteristics such as education, gender equality, and income, and we are trying to answer the question about how a certain score of these countries might impact the overall income, it is crucial to keep the data points of some countries that have much higher incomes, such as the USA, Switzerland, and Germany. To be able to answer the question, we need to observe more factors of these countries, which can give us insight into why there might be outliers. Simply put, you cannot find out more about something that you are trying to hide. Of course, this will inevitably lead to more errors from the model as a result, but this error can tell you more about the significance that the outliers have on the overall trend of your data, and how they can dictate how the outliers can have significance on awnsering your overall question.

What if you want a model that helps you find outliers compared to the overall trend in one glance? It turns out that there is a regression model created for exactly this purpose: support vector regression (SVR). This model uses the same mathematics behind multiple linear regression to plot the points but has a different way of displaying them, which can aid you in analyzing the data.

Support vector regression is named after support vectors, or vectors (data points that are defined by a value for units in x and y) that are at a certain distance from the general trendline of the dataset.

Points from which a trendline is drawn around the regression line of the dataset account for the range of values within a certain distance from the general trendline. The regression line is a line that shows the general level of increase among the y-values of the values in the dataset, but the trendline the support vectors make shows a boundary for how far, on average, the vectors are from the general trendline, forming a sort of pipe around it. The upper trendline accounts for the top 25 percent of points, and the bottom trendline accounts for the bottom 25 percent of points. Each of the new trendlines must have the same distance from the average trendline as the other to show the equal distance of the upper and lower ranges of values. Outliers, in this way, can be identified as values outside the space of the pipe, and the line can be adjusted with different values added to the dataset in the future on which the model is run.

All of this makes the support vector regression model a very wanted model for performing regression analysis on a dataset. The model performs a lot of the reasoning that you might need to do yourself to get a good picture of the data automatically. But how does this compare to linear and multivariate regression? Well, support vector regression uses the exact same equation as linear regression for producing the general trendline of the dataset, and it uses the exact same method of featuring the data points on a simple coordinate plane with a bunch of linear-style lines drawn through points. The difference comes from the calculation of the trendlines for the upper and lower range of points. The calculation is based on the range of values between the minimum and maximum value and what values are lower than 75 percent of the maximum value and greater than 50 percent of the maximum value of the dataset. For example, take a dataset with a maximum value of 100, and the values are [20, 30, 45, 67, 23, 46, 19, 23, 43, 34, 56, 78, 98]. The algorithm would first find the highest value in the dataset and it find 75 percent of what the value is. It would then draw a regression line through these values to mark this point on the graph, and this algorithm would do the same thing for the values that are 25 percent the greatest value in the dataset.

Knowing this, what if we are trying to answer questions where outliers play a significant part? Is there another metric we can use that does not give us the inflated errors of the mean squared error metric and the minimized error of the mean absolute squared metric? It turns out that there isn't a metric that is not fallible to outliers without having another kind of alternate issue which can alter the measurement of the error in one way or another. Mistakes in the world are just as prone to humans as errors are in statistics to mathematicians, and there is no way to fully avoid all of them.

For error metrics made for regression, there will always be a trade-off between a model that produces very sensitive error results, such as the mean squared error, and metrics that produce very small results like the mean absolute error. To measure the error in a regression model, we need to measure the error over the difference between each point in the model and the predicted value of this point, which requires measuring the error for every single point in the dataset (except for the y values or values we are trying to predict) and adding it up. When an error is added over and over again from a large set of numbers, the error will undoubtedly grow very large. When this happens, it either needs to be scaled to a certain range to be applicable to different kinds of values, or the error needs to be left the way it is to be able to perceive the error of all of the values in the dataset which leads to a bloated value, since there is no effort to minimize the error to fit the scale of the values in the dataset without getting rid of the outliers in the error measure to minimize the metric result.

Repeated calculations over and over again are much more prone to inflating errors, but what if instead of counting the distance between the points and the trendline of the graph for all the points we fed into our model to predict the result, we just count the number of wrong predictions and the number of right predictions? There isn't any way to inflate the number of errors a model can produce since it is only a percentage that increases with the same ratio of the number of right answers over wrong answers. The only tradeoff here is the fact that this metric cannot be used for measuring the error in regression models.

A Classification Accuracy

In regression models, when we are measuring the error, we are measuring the distance that is added up for all points in the dataset from their predicted value. Measuring how many assumptions were "incorrect" would not be possible since we do not have anything exactly from which to compare the distance of the regular y-value to the predicted y-value. When we are measuring the distance between the two values, we are not getting an accuracy as a response; we are receiving an error, which is describing the distance. A metric that describes the amount of correct and incorrect answers describes accuracy, not error. We only have one value that we need to use for deriving the value from.

For the models, we will go over in the next chapter, we will be predicting a value that will already be precise and will even be similar among all of them in problems using classification algorithms. With an actual value to compare the predicted value to, measuring the amount of right and wrong predictions is possible and can give us a very simple and meaningful insight into the accuracy of the metric.

This metric is called classification accuracy. It outputs four different measurements to describe the accuracy of predicted values: true positive, false positive, true negative, and false negative. Each one of these values is made up of a different calculation of certain values in the model over others, and the accuracy is measured with this metric by comparing one of the measurements, such as true positive, to the opposite measure of it, true negative. The results of the metric beginning with "true" measure the output of the metric that gives us insights into what these values represent, and the second part, such as "positive" and "negative," tells us whether they were predicted as correct or not.

True positive and false positive are values that represent the number of items that have been correctly identified. False positive and false negative values represent the number of items that have been incorrectly identified. Let's say that we are predicting whether, in a certain location, it has snowed or not in January last year. We can either answer yes or no to each question. Given this example, a true positive assumption would be saying that it has snowed in Antarctica in July last year. This is true since weather data shows that it has snowed for multiple weeks straight in Antarctica in January last year, and the assumption is positive since we have answered yes to the question we have been asked.

An example of a false positive is saying it has snowed on the beach in Hawaii in July last year. It is false since the assumption is incorrect, and it is positive since we have answered yes to the question of whether it has snowed in a certain location last year. A false negative can be saying that it has not snowed anywhere in Sweden last year in January. It is labeled false since the assumption is not correct that we have made, and it is negative since we have answered no to the question. Last of all, an assumption that is true negative can be saying it has not snowed in Dubai in the United Arab Emirates last year in January. This assumption is true since it is correct given the weather data we have, and it is negative since we have answered no to the question.

These simple insights are calculated by the number of answers that have been defined as correct over the number of total answers to split the results over the true and false spectrum, and it is further broken down by dividing the number of answers that were identified as true over the number of answers that are true, and vice versa for the true responses and the same for all of the true and the false responses. This simple insight can give us insight into how well the model gives us both the true and the false results from the classification. This metric will come in very handy for finding the accuracy of the next group of models that will be covered in the next chapter.

How Can We Classify That?

With the ability to perform linear regression, it is possible to answer very basic questions such as what the weather is going to be the next day in a stable climate location, and measure how well a model performed in predicting the results. But AI would be far from where it is today if this is all it could do. The world is full of all sorts of different problems, and knowing one approach to find insights is not enough if we would like AI to stand up to its real potential. What if we would like AI to be able to do more human-related and less computational-related tasks such as identifying what a watermelon looks like or trying to predict whether an online review for a product is good or bad? With regression as the only tool, we would not be able to come up with these kinds of responses. We need something different.

Classification algorithms are some of the oldest algorithms, along with the regression models, that actually began to be used for more humanlike tasks. What good is a thinking machine that can make a prediction about how much it is going to rain tomorrow if it can't even identify what rain is?

Classification tasks have all sorts of applications, including visual search (such as searching Google by an image of a certain item), identifying what is the mood of a certain piece of text (happy, sad, angry, neutral), and more. Classification algorithms relate to the way humans are able to bring meaning to an object to allow AI to do the same. Humans have the innate ability to give meaning to objects that might not have any big significance alone but have a certain use or functionality that gives them it. A computer cannot distinguish an orange from a pear unless it is first told what a pear and what an orange are. If you even want to make the algorithm more sophisticated, you can allow the computer to learn the functionality of an orange and a pear and also for the computer to be able to make more meaningful assumptions about these objects.

For AI to be able to learn the difference between the pear and the orange, the computer needs to have a label of a pear and an orange first to be able to identify what the pear is and what the orange is. The label can be anything from a description of what an orange is to a picture of an orange. It needs to be able to hold some kind of content that it can use to distinguish the difference between objects like a pear and an orange.

With this label, the algorithm is able to distinguish a pear from an orange and measure the accuracy using the classification accuracy metric, the error. When the model identifies an orange from a pear, the algorithm would tend to get a reward for a correct assumption and a punishment for a wrong assumption. Of course, this is not the kind of punishment that you might give to your dog if he makes a mess, but it is a metric in the model that decreases with every wrong result, simulating a punishment inside of the model.

Within the realm of machine learning, there are multiple types of classification models. Some of the most notable include support vector machines, naive Bayes, decision tree classification, and k-nearest neighbors. These types of algorithms can perform classification using any type of data except for images. Image data requires a specific type of processing in a certain type of algorithm, which we will learn about later, that allows it to extract the data from the image into a tight format that the model is able to process. For now, we will stick to just numerical and textual data to keep things simple.

The most basic classification model is the support vector machine for classification. We are already familiar with the same model used for regression, so what is the difference? The model still has the aspect of support vectors to keep its name, and that's the similarity. Its calculation for making assumptions for values is different, though. This model uses the use of support vectors for characterizing the boundaries between the categories of the values of different data points. Just like how the model creates a graph when used for regression based on support vectors that draw a line distinguishing the upper and lower ranges of values, it uses them to wrap the line distinguishing the difference of the classes of points based on certain data points. These support vectors will always leave space between the line distinguishing the classes and the data points relating to a specific class, and they can move this line depending on any new points, which might come closer to the line, pushing it to be closer to an exact distance between each of the classes of points.

To visualize this better, let's say we have a dataset that contains four different classes of fruits: pear, peach, apple, and grape. We have 500 total points with an equal amount of them belonging to a certain class, and we need to separate them equally on the graph to clearly see which data points are part of each class. Each of the data points has certain features that can help the model to distinguish what class they are a part of, such as color, place where they were grown, weight, and height.

The model will learn what weights, heights, and colors contribute to an apple and each of the other fruits and it will plot each new point on the graph given this information. When a point from another class like grapes is added to the graph, the line of distinction will be drawn between the data points that represent apples and grapes. The same will happen for pears and peaches along with the points of the classes that have already been mapped out onto the graph. From this point on, any points that have much more similar characteristics to data points of another class will be placed closer to the line of distinction. These will become the support vectors, and since there must be an equal amount of space between the line of distinction and the points on one side, the line distinguishing the classes is going to move in response.

In the model comparing the sorting of the data points into different fruits, a data point representing a pear that might come very close to the line of distinction and can become a support vector point in the model can have the color red, moving it closer to the other data points that represent a red fruit, the apple data points. As more and more points get added, those that come closer to the line than the ones that were already closer to the line will become the new support vectors, and they will push the line into a new shape. This assures that the line always finds the exact center of the points when the process of the model making the distinctions between the classes is finished and the result is graphed to show the best possible separation of the points from the different classes.

But what about lines of distinction that cross over each other? In the fruit classification model, we have four different categories of fruits. This will mean that no matter how the points or the lines are arranged in the coordinate plane, the lines will always cross over. So what would this mean for the support vectors? Well, the support vectors might increase in amount with the points crammed up into a smaller region of the graph. More of them will be closer to the line of distinction between the different classes of points. It won't amount to anything more than a very tightly fitted graph with points, but you will always be assured that the line of distinction will be fitted as well as possible in the intersection between the different classes. This makes the model a very good choice for organizing very messy data in a clear, readable way since support vector machine models are great to be used when it comes down to asking for a clear separation between the classes. With other classification models, the line of separation will not always be very clear and can curve around other points in the other class.

A great use of a support vector machine model can be for recognizing a cancerous tumor primarily because images taken of tumors up close can be very messy when it comes to recognizing what parts of the images hold values that relate to the outline of a tumor in the image. For finding outliers, though, this model might be a poor choice. Along with it also comes the problem of a lot of time it takes to train the model. So what can be some other options for classification if we would like a quicker, organized way of displaying data?

If you have data with more outliers that you would like to have organized in a better manner, why not choose to group it up with the points it is closest to instead of changing the boundary between the classes of points? It is a naive option after all. Why should you force a point to be part of a certain class instead of changing the boundary between the classes of the points that it is surrounded with and making it clearer? So it would make sense that this is what the naive Bayes algorithm was made to do. This algorithm is made for organizing data with more outliers using the tactics we have outlined above and creates a rather messy division between the classes the points are sorted into.

The naive Bayes algorithm gets its name from the calculation it is based on: Bayes' theorem. This theorem is used to find the probability of two events occurring at the same time by taking the probability of the second event over the first event, multiplying it by the probability of the first event, and dividing this by the probability of the second event occurring. Doing this will give you the probability of the first event occurring when the second event occurs. This operation can also be done to find the probability of the first event over the second event, but you need to know the probability of the first event over the second event first. But how can this theorem possibly be used for grouping up the points together? Well, the output of this operation is a probability of the first event occurring over the second event, knowing the probability of each event individually occurring and the second event occurring over the first. This probability is used to estimate whether a certain data point should belong to a specific class of points. If the probability that one point belongs to a certain class over another, the point is placed into the class that it has the higher probability of belonging to. If a point has a 56 percent chance of belonging to a class of red points and a 44 percent chance of belonging to the class of blue points, the point is placed into the class of red points. This is the reason why in graphs of the output of this algorithm there can be very little overlap seen between the two classes of points. If there is one point that has even a 49 percent chance of belonging to the blue group and a 51 percent chance of belonging to the red class, the point will still be placed into the red class. This one percent difference is the reason for the point when graphed in the result of this model being on the edge of the two classes.

This is why this model is very good for datasets with a lot of outliers. The outliers, as we have mentioned before, can be distinguished no matter how similar they are to another class in the class to which they belong. This is also the reason why a line does not need to be put in place to separate the different classes from each other. It is not going to be a line for that one value with the one percent difference of belonging to the other class placed in such close proximity to the other class of points that it creates a curve in it. Secondly, a line is not part of the calculation of the algorithm and would not do a good job of showing that some of the points from the other class are in that specific class with unclear representation, to begin with, the distinction of the points in the classes.

The algorithm has applications in many basic classification tasks, similar to the tasks that support vector machines are used in, with the difference of the types of datasets this model processes its data from. The data that the naive Bayes model processes can be data that might not produce a very accurate result using the support vector machine given the big differences both models have. Applications that also involve determining a result based on probability are heavily used with this algorithm. Some notable applications of naive Bayes in the real world include recommendation algorithms (YouTube video recommendation algorithm, Facebook feed recommendation algorithm) and filtering out email spam.

But what if we don't want to base our results on probabilities specifically, and we would like it to be done in a more systematic way such as how we did in regression with decision trees? It turns out we can do the same for classification!

Decision Trees in Classification

Decision trees also have a unique variation for classification problems. Decision trees have applications in many parts of machine learning, including regression and classification. The idea they are based on allows their calculations to be used very easily across many different parts of machine learning. Decision trees used for classification are called decision tree classification. The idea behind this algorithm is no different from the decision trees used for regression; it is only what it is comparing that is different.

Decision trees in regression work by comparing the features of a specific data point to those that precede it in the dataset. Each decision about the next data point is used to make decisions about the data point after it, allowing it to have a flow that creates an assumption about grouping up the data. We have seen this in action when we described a flowchart that helps you determine what generation you are part of based on your age. But decision trees for classification work in a different way. When we use decision trees for classification, we are still comparing the values of the data like weight or height, but we are sorting the data into classes for the result. This allows for easy classification between multiple classes at the same time, unlike in the support vector machine model, where this kind of distinction can lead to a messy result. In our decision tree, all we need to do is simply "branch the tree out," and we can include more results from certain ways of grouping up the data.

This method seems like it is meant for a perfectly classified result with as many classes as possible! Well, it can be effective specifically when it comes down to classification, but what about if we have a dataset with points that belong to many different classes? What if, in fact, that number is huge? Maybe we have a dataset with one hundred different classes? It is not impossible that this exists. After all, we are finding out more each month about our planet, and as we learn more, we have to consider more things when making a decision and more possible opportunities leading to more outcomes. So are we going to have to wait all day long to get a result from our model? At a certain point, we might end up needing to wait this long, but we can certainly speed it up.

With one hundred or more classes, a decision tree is going to become *huge*. But is it possible to make the time it takes to compute the results from this model faster? Well, yes! What if, instead of having only one giant decision tree to branch out into all the possible events that we need to account for using our dataset, we use multiple different decision trees at the same time? What if we use an entire forest of them? Unsurprisingly, this method is called decision forests, and they can also be used for regression purposes.

A random forest is a version of the decision tree model with just many different trees working together to lower the amount of processing time for the model. The way this model works is that there are multiple decision trees created out of the single decision tree modeled specifically for the application, and different parts of the data are sent to one of these trees in the decision forest model. This allows the computational time to go down since, instead of pushing all data down the same tree, the same calculations can be made on different trees at the same time. But at the expense of this comes the accuracy of the model. The accuracy of each decision tree slides the less data it is being used on, with less training that the tree is doing with the data of the entire set. The more trees used in the forest model means the less accurate each of the trees is.

There is always a tradeoff between one advantage and another disadvantage, and this instance is the most common: speed versus accuracy. Speed and accuracy are sort of opposites in a way, even when it comes to human learning itself. If a human were measured on the amount of time for them to complete a test compared to if they were measured on accuracy, the result of the test measured for speed would be much less accurate than the test measured for accuracy. If you are trying to sort items into different categories, you will do a better job when you can think more thoroughly about in which categories to place the objects, and having less time lessens this opportunity. So what is better depends on your situation: do you want a more accurate model that can take more time to perform or a model that is much faster to run but takes longer?

The most popular answer to this debate is simply using a model that takes a longer time to perform but is more accurate when accuracy is highly important in the result, such as medical imaging. Also, larger datasets usually produce more inaccurate results in any machine learning model anyway, so why not just speed up the amount of time it takes to execute? It is common sense, after all, to group data where the accuracy rating is very important into smaller batches to be processed.

The Most Basic Classification Algorithm

We have already learned about many different models, including support vector machines (SVM), naive Bayes, and decision trees. But what about a model that is so simple and intuitive that it would be foolish not to think of it yourself at the very beginning of computer science history? Think about how you would group a bunch of items. You would first start by knowing how many classes there are to group the items into, then you would group them by the similarity of features such as color, and whenever a new point comes in, you would do the same for that.

But what if you did not have any features for these points? What if you only had them scattered around, and you knew how many sections you needed to group them into? In this way, you would group the first few points into the group that is closest to them by distance, creating the different classes in the dataset. Do this for all of the items you need to sort, and eventually, you will have sorted out all of the items in your dataset. This is what the algorithm we will go over next does. It is called k-nearest neighbors, or KNN for short.

The name comes from its functionality of grouping points given their distance to another group of points. The k letter comes from a way to represent a number of classes to group the points into, sort of like a variable in math such as x. Knowing this, you can probably guess what the two n letters in the name stand for. This method is the most basic method for performing classification in machine learning due to its very straightforward nature. This algorithm uses distance as the main determiner of whether a point should be grouped in a certain group or not, but it is important to note the different types of distances that this algorithm can use.

Distance in Graphing

There are different ways of measuring distance on a graph. The most straightforward method is called Euclidean distance. It is the most popular metric for measuring distance due to its simplicity. It is calculated by adding the differences between the x- and y-values of each point squared and taking the square root of this number. More specifically, the difference is taken between the x-values for both points and squared, and this number is added to the same operation done with the y-values. Only after this is the square root is taken. This metric is most commonly used with the k-nearest neighbors model.

If you would prefer something different, the other option for you is called Manhattan distance. The name does not come from the fact that the mathematician who came up with it lives in Manhattan. It is called this way after the fact that it measures distance across a graph across the squares on it. The Euclidean distance measures the distance in a diagonal line, but the Manhattan distance measures the distance across the squares in a diagonal line. This formula was created for taxi cab drivers to model on a map how to reach one block that is a straight diagonal distance away from them on a map. They try to optimize the amount of time they spend on a certain route over another to be able to earn the best amount of profit, and so they need to know the distance from one point to another on a map in terms of the streets it takes to get there (especially in a city) to do this. They cannot just drive through the buildings in the cities to get to the location, so they need to get the distance to get to that location in terms of the number of blocks it takes to get there. This kind of metric is used much less due to the higher complexity of its calculation and due to the nature of the calculation. If you aren't drawing a line on a graphed sheet of paper, this method becomes more difficult to visualize and interpret. Although both methods will be very important in the next chapter.

By now, you probably assume that classification models are a wondrous part of machine learning that provides a very basic but crucial skill for any brain to have. However, we still have not yet learned everything we need to understand how almost all modern AI tools work. With only the knowledge for predicting results from labeled datasets, AI would still be very limited today. If artificial intelligence is supposed to mimic human learning, we would need for there to be more automated reasoning going on inside of the algorithm. Young children only walk around the house for so long to ask their parents what an apple and a pear are. They eventually will need to learn how to distinguish items without knowing explicitly what they are called. With such advanced algorithms that run our lives nowadays, there needs to be a way to allow a computer to learn without labels and simply to go off on its own with knowledge about the data it is supposed to predict and find out the patterns itself.

Cluster Up!

What algorithm can answer the question we have posed? What if we have a classification task for the model to perform? If we try an algorithm like *k*-nearest neighbors to perform this task, it will make a mess out of its results, trying to hallucinate something it can't see. Or what about multiple linear regression? How can it plot what it cannot see? Is there a way to configure these algorithms to allow them to see patterns from the data and not require labels to be present in the data for these algorithms to work? The answer is that none of these algorithms can.

Algorithms within the atmosphere of machine learning can be split into two different categories: supervised and unsupervised learning. As we already know, supervised learning is about aiding the model in predicting the results by giving it the correct results to actively compare the current results to. These algorithms are constructed to depend on data labels to be able to learn from the data. The latter involves allowing the model to learn all by itself the correct answers for the data.

So far, we have only looked at the environments for regression and classification in machine learning. This environment contains only supervised learning models. The functionality of these algorithms requires them to have a correct result to compare their summarized result to. The ability for an algorithm to visualize the pattern within data must be built within the basis behind the algorithm to begin with. For example, the k-nearest neighbors algorithm needs to have labeled categories for which the points need to be separated instead of comparing the properties of the data points and uncovering similarities from the data in that way.

Supervised vs Unsupervised Learning

One way to think about this is the difference between a cat and a dog walking around your house at night. Both cats and dogs have night vision, so they are able to walk around your house at night and not bump into your couch. However, when it comes to climbing on the furniture and finding a great place to sleep for the night, the cat is more likely to get the best spot. Cats have better night vision than dogs and are more nimble, so they can much more easily navigate around the space than the dog would. While in the morning you can find your cat cozied up inside an open kitchen cupboard taking a nap, the dog will probably be napping on the ground next to your dining table.

In a similar way to a cat and a dog navigating around your house at night, you can also think of unsupervised machine learning models as being like a cat, more nimble at spotting differences, and having greater independence to come up with their own results. On the other hand, supervised learning models are more limited; they require you to give them instructions on what to do. Just like how the night vision of a dog is more limited than that of a cat, supervised learning models cannot see as many insights from the data as unsupervised learning models can. But that doesn't mean that unsupervised models are superior to supervised learning models in every way.

As we have already seen, there is always a tradeoff in the world of AI between one benefit and another for a certain downfall, such as the tradeoff of accuracy for speed. With the amazing benefits of unsupervised learning models not having any ropes to walk on when it crosses the bridge to give you the answers you need, they sometimes can make a wrong turn, walk off it, and produce some mistakes, such as through hallucinating patterns. Supervised learning algorithms overall produce higher accuracy rates than unsupervised learning algorithms, with having the labels as undeniably correct results. The labels are the guardrails on the bridge, making it much harder for the algorithm to accidentally walk off it.

For determining the risks associated with using a model with one benefit over another, it is important to realize the situation we are using the model. Unsupervised models are the basis for large AI algorithms like ChatGPT, which can come up with insights simply by conglomerating more data from the Internet and answers to more people asking questions. If a machine learning model is made for commercial use or for the use of simply being out there for people to use, we need the algorithm to be able to gather insights from data that might be very disconnected from the data it was originally trained on.

So what if in our case we would like to create a model that can split into groups a large dataset of customer profiles given attributes to find out what their shopping habits are and what kinds of ads we would like to show them for our product? Luckily for us, we don't have to create this algorithm; a family of them, in fact, already exists. These algorithms are called clustering algorithms. They are made to solve the same kinds of problems that classification algorithms are made to solve but with data without labels. We don't need to already know the categories of ads to show specific customers. If we had already known this information to begin with, we wouldn't even need to run this model to get it. All we need to know are just the most basic features of each of the customers to allow our algorithm to find the pattern out for itself.

As from the example, you can probably already guess what the applications of this algorithm are. They can be for any task when it comes to doing what classification algorithms can do but without labeled data. This makes the purpose of these algorithms perfect for being used in the real world for the purpose of doing analysis on large batches (sets) of data. When a dataset is large enough, no one would bother to put labels on thousands of values, so even for handling large sets of data, this algorithm is also optimal. The features of clustering make it a type of machine learning model that is much closer to the human brain than others so was a large advancement in the field of AI for its time.

As with all families of algorithms we have seen so far, clustering algorithms also come in their own flavors. One of these flavors is *k*-means, similar to the classification algorithm but recreated to be used without labeled data, another algorithm with a similar structure as decision trees, where each decision about where to place the next point is based on decisions about the last. Additionally, there is a clustering algorithm with a unique way of grouping the data with even the most minimal amount of information provided, even to an unsupervised algorithm, and an algorithm that is made for finding outliers and making its calculations based on the density of the clusters.

There are many different types of algorithms to choose from within this section that have a particularly unique method of processing data when building a model. For the example above, we can use any of these models for producing a meaningful result about the different categories of ads to show our customers, and given whether we know already how many categories of ads to show the customers to begin with, we already can begin to think about what type of algorithm we would like to use.

Within any field of machine learning, there are numerous different algorithms, each created during a different time span and for a different purpose. Some of the algorithms were even built on top of other algorithms that span across multiple machine learning domains, such as the decision tree algorithm. To find the algorithm that is best suited for a certain problem, it is best to know about all the data that there is for the problem and the task we would like our algorithm to perform. If outliers are a big concern, we should use an algorithm that is optimized for handling outliers smoothly. If we are unsure about how many different categories we would like our model to group the data into, this is another factor that we need to consider when we choose the model. While the models can be configured for different inputs the overall internal structure of the model cannot be changed. It is wise to choose a model to stick with to solve all of the problems inside the dataset to begin with than to choose a less suitable model and configure a model to do perform better after many incorrect results were obtained.

With this in mind, let's begin exploring the options on our table for how we can solve the problem of finding the types of ads to show the customers. To get a clear introduction to this domain, let's start with k-means clustering.

What exactly is k-means clustering? The name is similar to k-nearest neighbors, and this is intentional. Both algorithms are based on the same underlying system: grouping up the data points into k amounts of groups. The primary difference between the two algorithms is the simple fact that k-means clustering is the clustering version of k-nearest neighbors, and it does not require labeled data. In a similar way to how a decision tree model can be used for regression and classification purposes, k-based models can be used for two different types of data. The version we are going to be exploring is a version created specifically for the purpose of clustering and unsupervised learning.

Similar to k-nearest neighbors, the intuition for the structure of this algorithm is very straightforward. It simply is an algorithm to group data into a k amount of groups and to do this until all the points are grouped into the neatest clusters with no points overlapping between any of the groups. This algorithm does this through repetition of reassigning points to different groups and changing up existing groups to match the new change. The algorithm initializes k amount of points which become centers of groups or clusters of points, and depending on the distance between one of these clusters, a point is assigned to the cluster it is closest to by a measure of Euclidean distance. A single point that can be caught within two groups can misplace an entire group, causing large errors in results. So this algorithm can go over dozens of iterations of regrouping the points before settling on the best output possible. It, of course, cannot be the absolute perfect answer, though, because the points can be infinitely closer to another group.

It can be shocking to think about it, but because our numerical system is infinite on both the positive and negative ends, the measurements that we make can never be as precise as possible. If you try measuring a pen with a ruler, you will probably only round to the nearest centimeter or tick mark on the specific measuring device you are using. If your pen, for example, is forty-seven centimeters long and the tip of it is caught in between the upper and lower bound measure, you will need to imagine a tick mark to represent half of the distance between these two marks. Depending on whether the tip of the pen is under or over the mark will determine whether the pen is forty-seven or forty-six centimeters long. But that is not all. If you would like to get a measurement that is measured in tenths of centimeters, then you need to make your margin of measurement even smaller. You will need to add an extra seven ticks along with the original benchmark tick, but what if the pen tip still falls between one of those measurements? You can minimize the margin of error further and further by zooming closer into the distance between the tip and the tick, and no matter how much you keep zooming in, you will never be able to get to exactly the point where the tick matches perfectly the measure of the pen tip. This is the same analogy as the *k*-means clustering algorithm.

The algorithm will continue to iterate by changing the centers of the different clusters of points again and again until it is visually observable that there are no points intersecting between groups. Of course, due to the computer's incredibly fast speed of performing computations through the CPU, it isn't apparent how much work the computer is actually doing underneath the surface. But in models we will explore later, the computational time will drastically increase.

K-means clustering can be applied to any clustering problem and can produce a very visually appealing output. If we were to train this algorithm on the example problem of grouping customers into certain categories to show ads to, we would initialize the variable k to be the number of ads we are going to show to our customers. We will set the distance to be determined by Euclidean distance for simplicity purposes, and this model will run through our dataset looking for similarities between different customers for factors such as age, location, and language. Given these categories, we would have an output that would match a customer who is the same age and in the same location but who speaks a different language than another customer into the same group as a customer who is the same age and in the same location.

This seems like an intuitive way to easily solve the problem of grouping customers into different categories, but does it produce any specific errors? Well, as mentioned before, every single model in machine learning does produce some kind of error that is based on the structure of the algorithm. So let's see what might not be good use cases for this model. To start off, obviously, if you don't know what the value of k is, then this would be a problem since this algorithm relies on knowing the number of groups to sort the data into beforehand. Secondly, a dataset with outliers might ruin the accuracies of all other data points in the set by misleading the algorithm into moving the center points of the clusters toward them. In this sense, this algorithm might not be very suitable for the problem of grouping customers for ads. A customer dataset is likely to have many outliers, so k-means clustering might make many mistakes there.

DBSCAN is another algorithm is machine learning for clustering, which has a slightly different method for clustering that can aid in finding outliers. DBSCAN has a similar intuition to k-means clustering, involving grouping points around a center point of a cluster that it is closest to, but there is one major difference. This difference can also be an answer to a question centered around making a clustering algorithm made for outliers: What if instead of having k number of unique clusters, we have a minimum number of points inside each cluster, and clusters with the minimum amount of points are put inside the middle while those that have less than the minimum number of points are put on the outside? It might not be the most straightforward answer, but it certainly does work.

The clusters that are part of the same category overlap in their range, allowing them to shade a larger part of the graph for specific points to join. This method can very effectively minimize the number of outliers by having more clusters than in the k-means algorithm, which forces more points to join an existing cluster rather than pull a cluster that already exists closer toward it. To be able to use it, you need to know the eps, which is the minimum radius any neighboring points around a center point can be placed within, and the minimum number of points for a cluster. A high value for the eps leads to more of the data being placed into isolated clusters, and a lower value for the eps indicates the data being grouped up into barely any clusters at all. In this case, the data will be mostly randomized. The minimum number of points indicates the minimum number of data points that can be placed within the radius value described by eps. This allows the algorithm to minimize the effect of outliers through the effect of pushing points toward a median in the data.

With the additional pro of being able to minimize the effect of error from outliers, this algorithm also allows you to see the categories into which most of the points fall. For our example above, this would be a great algorithm to use in the case of not knowing how many advertisements we would like to show our customers. If we are using a DBSCAN model for our example, we first need to choose a value for the eps, which can allow our data to be clustered just enough to be able to get as neat of an output as the k-means clustering algorithm but not as distantly spaced so we have outliers like in the *k*-means clustering algorithm. The eps value will need to be adjusted over time to get a good enough value to make sure that the clusters are the right size, along with changing the minimum number of points. The best value to begin with for the minimum number of points is 3, and from there, we can measure the results to tweak this value and the eps to optimize the model.

Along with DBSCAN and *k*-means clustering, there are still other models that are great to know about for certain datasets where DBSCAN and *k*-means clustering might not deliver great results. One of these models is the Gaussian mixture algorithm, and it may sound by the name that this algorithm requires a lot of math, but it is similar to the other kinds of algorithms in the mathematics behind its functioning. The Gaussian mixture algorithm is one of the only clustering algorithms that can deal with noncircular data. Clusters within the DBSCAN and *k*-means clustering algorithms require data with few outliers to be able to group them into a circular format. The Gaussian mixture algorithm can help cluster data into a noncircular shape to fit data with many outliers in a neat way.

With these clustering algorithms, we can effectively teach our computer to group the points in any dataset. With knowledge of a much more automated algorithm for performing clustering, we can now look at algorithms which are at the base of models like ChatGPT. All the models we have covered so far are much more basic in their functionality compared to today's date and are used as the backbone for many more basic algorithms. Now we need to learn about the algorithms behind what everyone is talking about.

Learning Deeply

What is it that makes ChatGPT so smart? We have learned so far about all kinds of algorithms, those that can allow computers to group objects up, identify them, and predict the next value in a sequence of points, but none of these algorithms can make a machine as intelligent the way that the algorithm behind ChatGPT does. So what can? It obviously needs to be different from any we have learned so far. It needs to be as similar as possible to how the human brain is structured to process data in such a neat and orderly manner.

The human brain is made up of neurons that pulse electrical signals, also called action potentials, through our brains. The neurons are connected by synapses, and different arrangements of them allow information to be processed in different ways through different parts of our brains. There is a different part of our brain for controlling different tasks, such as visual perception (seeing things with our eyes) and motion that allows our brain to connect to different body parts. The same goes for the network that ChatGPT is based on. ChatGPT, as of the writing of this book, has the functionality to scan images and process text synchronously. The network that ChatGPT is based on is called an artificial neural network (ANN), which is part of a family of algorithms called neural networks, modeled directly after the structure of the human brain. These algorithms are so unique in comparison to the algorithms in classification, regression, and clustering that they even are part of a different branch of AI called deep learning.

The ANN network has nodes that can hold information, similar to the neurons in our brain, and it connects to other neurons to transfer data to them to get an insight based on this data through a basic mathematical equation such as the equation of a line: $wx + b$.

The W in this equation represents the weight, which is a number assigned through a method called gradient descent (which we will go over later) for a neuron in a neural network, and the b stands for the bias value. The bias value is generated based on the output of a function depending on the type of input you have to the network. This value is then transferred to all of the neurons in the layer after it. There can be many layers of these neurons inside a neural network, and at the end of the neural network, there is always an output layer, or a layer which is the layer that determines the output of the network. The number of neurons in the output layer of the model is determined by the number of categories the model has to output. For example, a model that outputs a binary value (0 or 1) will need only two neurons for the output layer.

This all sounds straightforward, but how can this algorithm make software like ChatGPT so intelligent? It doesn't seem like anything within this algorithm is very special. If you are thinking this way right now, you are not alone. Many people, when they are first introduced to deep learning, wonder exactly how does this type of algorithm create such accurate outcomes to certain problems. The answer to this question is not very simple. It is generally all parts of the ANN that need to work together in sync to create the complex output that we see as the user as the end, but the specific part of the neural network that is probably most responsible for this intelligent output is the function that provides the value for the bias, otherwise called the activation function. This function is what determines the uniqueness of the value of each neuron in the network from the $wx + b$ equation and the type of input given to the network, along with the output.

In the example of a binary classifier that we would like to make with an ANN, the neurons in the layers between the input layer and the output layer, called the hidden layers, are most probably going to use a binary step function (also known as a ReLU function), which is a function that always generates a value from 0 to 1. When rounded up, it is one of the two, so when we use this for our hidden neurons in the network, we will get a value that will indicate which outcome a certain neuron thinks about the outcome. The graph of this function, when plotted, shows a line representing this function that jumps at a linear rate from the value of 0 to the value of 1. This function begins from 0 since it does not encompass any negative values. If our classifier is classifying pictures of cats from dogs, then a 1 output from a neuron might indicate that the image is of a cat, and a 0 for an image of a dog. This is the most simplistic step function within the neural network for predicting certain output values, but if we have a more complex dataset with more than two output values, we will need different types of functions.

There are many different types of functions that can be used for neural networks with more than two outputs, but the most common are the sigmoid logistic function, softmax, and the leaky ReLU. The logistic sigmoid function can take outputs from between and including values from 0 to 1. This function can be used optimally for problems where we would have a probability output ranging from more precise values such as 0.45 and 0.325. The softmax function, in this regard, is very similar. Just like the sigmoid logistic function, the softmax function can output values between 0 and 1, but there is a very important difference with this function. The sigmoid and the softmax functions are most widely used in the output layer of the ANN due to their ability to produce very precise values for output in comparison to other activation functions. The values of the sigmoid function stay independent from one another, meaning one value that the sigmoid function outputs does not influence the next value that the sigmoid function outputs, whereas the values that the softmax function outputs always need to sum to one.

The context of which is more correct would depend on your problem, such as predicting whether a day is rainy, sunny, or cloudy. These events are intertwined by one another. If we are trying to predict the weather of a given day only given by the weather of past days, we will need to give the model we need to tell our model that the events are dependent on one another. If we are predicting the weather by the day, and not by the hour of the day then we only will have three options given by our input for what the weather of the day can be: rainy, sunny, or cloudy. A day that is rainy cannot also be sunny, at least not by the time range of the entire day, and a day that is sunny could decrease the chance of a day being rainy, while a day that is cloudy can increase the chance of the next day being rainy. So if we are predicting whether a day is rainy, sunny, or cloudy, we would need each value to be dependent on each other and all three probabilities to add up to 1.

A sigmoid function used for this problem, on the other hand, would produce values that are independent of each other, and while given their results would be accurate for function output they would not make any sense for the problem. A day that has a 0.67 chance of rain cannot have a 0.80 chance of being sunny. The same sigmoid function, though, may be useful if we are trying to predict the weather for seven days rather than one day with our three conditions. A day that is 0.80 chance sunny cannot influence the next day being also 0.80 percent chance rainy. Conditions in the weather very easily change from one day to the next (especially in some parts of the world more than others), so it is important to know the problem before you begin building your neural network and choosing your activation functions.

Some problems can be very unique and may have a very tight requirement for the type of output. Another problem situation that may arise is a problem where there is a pure 0 or 1 without rounding. For this problem, we would use the binary step function. The binary step function is the same in the way of outputting a 0 or 1, just like the ReLU function, but different in that any value that the function outputs that is not zero is 1, and any number that is zero is, well, zero. This does not allow for a lot of room in calculations and can be a great function to use in cases where there is not a need for a precise answer to a calculation.

Learning

It is very noticeable to see how much of the accuracy of the results depends on the activation functions, but how does the neural network actually learn? Activation functions are a part of the network that needs to be initialized at the beginning and do not change throughout the course of training the neural network. So what does it do automatically to help itself learn? For this answer, we need to look back at the human brain and how it learns.

The best way athletes prepare for sporting events is by repeating moves over and over again. Why? Think of an athlete who wants to master a certain move in their sport for an upcoming sporting event. To train, the athlete performs the movement over and over again to get their body used to doing the move over and over again, and certain muscles in their body become stronger to be able to witstand doing this move. The brain, which is responsible for communicating with different parts of the body to perform this move, rewires itself every time it performs the move again. The more the athlete practices the move, the more the neurons in their brain become accustomed to connecting to delivering the electrical pulses to the other neurons in the brain. The connections between certain neurons grow stronger over time as the athlete repeats the movement they want to practice.

This is a very similar process to what happens inside a neural network when being trained. The neural network takes a certain amount of data called batches that it trains the neural network on for by pushing the data through the network, applying the $f(x) = wx + b$ equation to the input data, where x is a piece of the data that is being pushed through the neural network. The value for $f(x)$ is then pushed to the next neuron it connects to and added to the value of this function from the other neurons in the same layer. When the data reaches a neuron in the next layer of the neural network, it continues through the entire network.

After the data goes through the entire network, there is an accuracy rating that the network receives about how well the network did in predicting the output for all of the data. After receiving this value, the network will change its weights (which is the w value in the equation) and push another batch of the data through the network. This process is called backpropagation, and it is another feature that allows the neural network to produce very intelligent conclusions about complex problems. This will be done for a certain amount of times called epochs. Depending on the type of data being processed through the neural network, the amount of epochs, the RAM of the computer you are running the network on, and the batch size, the neural network can take sometimes fifteen minutes to go through a training process.

Accuracy ratings can be displayed differently depending on the programming language the model is made in. With the Keras library in the Python programming language (currently the world's most popular programming language), which is one of the most widely used libraries for making deep learning algorithms, there are usually statistics showing the accuracy of the network after all of the training has been completed. These include the accuracy rating per epoch, the total accuracy, and the loss of the neural network (predicted using the same functions as machine learning models, such as mean squared error). Values that will be only shown after the neural network is fully finished training are the value loss and value accuracies. The value loss and accuracies are the same as the general accuracies and losses for the model.

Optimization

If you are like most people, and you don't want to wait fifteen minutes or more for a simple neural network to finish training, then there are ways to modify it to train quicker. Increasing the batch size of the network helps more pieces of data to be processed through the network, which allows the neural network to be processed faster. The amount of epochs also dictates the speed of the neural network training. The more epochs you would like the model to take to learn from the data, the more time it will take for the neural network to finish training. Depending on the model that you are using and its base configurations, each model will need to be changed in a different way to achieve a lesser running time or more accurate values.

Another big difference between machine learning and deep learning is that the tradeoff between time and accuracy is not always the case in deep learning as it is in machine learning. Sometimes configurations to a model that increase its accuracy can also decrease the amount of time it takes for the model to run! It just comes down to knowing the problem that you are trying to solve well and knowing all of the parts of the neural network you have made and how they interact together to be able to come up with a configuration that will achieve both a timely and accurate result.

Other parts of a neural network that can also be configured include the number of layers the neural network has, the learning rate, and the layer units. The learning rate controls how fast the neural network learns from the data. The learning rate controls a process of the neural network called gradient descent, which controls the weights of the neural network. Remember how the weights of the neural network are changed after every epoch the network is trained with? This happens through gradient descent, which is a process that includes the weights of the neural network being repetitively adjusted to be able to find a local minimum. A higher learning rate of the neural network increases the learning rate of the network by changing the weights by a larger increment to try to find the local minimum. A learning rate that is too high, though, might also cause your network to overfit values, so it is best to adjust the learning rate by a little bit if you need the network to run faster or have a higher accuracy. Increasing the size of each of the layers can be a better option for increasing the accuracy of the neural network without a risk of overfitting.

The size of each layer corresponds to the number of nodes, which corresponds to the number of neurons in a layer of the network. Usually, more neurons in a layer can mean a higher accuracy for the model. Since each neuron in each layer creates its own calculation with the equation $wx + b$, it makes another assumption that can be passed on to the next layer, increasing the chance of the output of the next layer to include a correct assumption. The number of layers, on the other hand, includes the number of groups of neurons in a neural network that the data needs to be passed through until it reaches the output. Increasing the number of layers similarly also increases the number of assumptions that can be made with the data from the equation for each neuron. It also gives you the opportunity to add more activation functions to the neural network with each extra layer you add, which allows your network to make more particular assumptions based on the features in the data. It is best to note that while adding more layers and layer units is a great way to increase the accuracy of your network, it is also best to increment slowly, just as with changing the learning rate. Switching from a value such as five layers for the neural network to ten might actually hurt the accuracy of the neural network. Too much or too little of anything is bad.

It is now clear to see why a model like ChatGPT can be built on a model such as a neural network for all of the complex assumptions it can make on so many different topics. Models as large as ChatGPT or Google's LaMDA can have millions of nodes and tens of thousands of different layers all put together into one giant model. But ChatGPT, apart from being able to make rational assumptions on thousands of different topics, is also able to reason with pictures. Recently, ChatGPT has released a functionality to be able to produce output from a given image for solving a problem inside of it. One person gave ChatGPT a picture of his bike seat, explained the problem he was facing (which was the bike seat being too high), and asked it how to fix it. ChatGPT, from this image, outputs a response tailored to the exact bike the person had, explaining how to fix it step by step.

You might now be wondering: *How could we have gone over almost everything about the machine and deep learning but not how images are processed?* Image recognition in the field of artificial intelligence is such a big topic that it has its own part of the field called computer vision. Computer vision is a field of AI just like machine learning and deep learning that is focused on the processing of different images in different ways. If you have ever used a Snapchat filter, you have used a computer vision algorithm firsthand. Snapchat filters use real-time motion detection algorithms to identify parts of your face to place certain parts of a certain animal, such as a dog. It does this hundreds of times a second scanning your face and identifying different points on your face such as your eyes, nose, and mouth, and placing the part of the dog filter appropriate for certain parts of the face on the locations of these points on the screen. After you make a movement, the algorithm goes back to reidentify the parts of your face and replace the parts of the filter in the new locations. Since all of these calculations are happening so fast, you as the user would barely notice anything, but inside your device, there are billions of calculations going on, and depending on how many calculations the software you are using with this kind of functionality on, computers with eight gigabytes of RAM or less might begin to lag or crash. All of these calculations are made possible by the computer being able to identify parts of your face and put all of these parts together into the whole image of your face. This is the core of how computer vision works.

Computer vision, while being part of a different section of AI than deep learning, has its roots within the field of deep learning for being able to perform this functionality. Remember how ANNs are part of a family of algorithms called neural networks, and different algorithms within this family are built on top of the artificial neural network? Well, there is a model that is the equivalent of an ANN that can recognize images, which is responsible for any kind of image recognition within the field of deep learning called a CNN (convolutional neural network). Any kind of algorithm within the field of deep learning that does image recognition is used or is built on top of this algorithm. The algorithm is named this way after the most basic neural network, the artificial neural network, which it is built on top of, and the definition of convolution, which means to be able to make larger images smaller by taking segments of them and rebuilding the images in a different way to allow them to be processed by the neural network.

Within the CNN, the convolutional element comes before the beginning of the ANN. When an image is run through a CNN model, it is first split into many different equal parts. From these parts of the image, different values are extracted based on the features present in the image. These features can include parts of the image. For example, in a black and white image, a segment of the picture that is taken, when split up into multiple different boxes, will have either the color black or white mostly in each box. Boxes that are mostly black can be represented with a zero, and boxes that are mostly white can be represented as a one. Then the numbers of 1s and 0s taken from each different image segment can be added up together and can be visualized in a new charted graph, a sum of the number of zeros and ones for each different segment of the total image grouped together. This process can continue to repeat for all segments of the full image until all of the image has been broken up into different segments which have been broken up into parts, given values for these parts, and summed into a new format.

After each step, you will notice that the image we are dealing with will shrink in size. This is the point of what convolution is supposed to accomplish. The computer cannot process full-scale images directly in the neural network. As we already know, neural networks and other kinds of AI models require numerical data to perform calculations to interpret patterns and reach a conclusion. Images alone, if they were to be represented by the red-blue-green (RGB) numerical values, even in their numerical forms, would not be in a compressed enough format to run through the network. Data from a dataset that we run through our network is ordered by columns and rows, and RGB values alone are too large in quantity even for a simple colored image, and do not have a good enough way of being represented to be entered into the neural network. Convolution aims to rid the image of its complexity and fit it into a numerical vector that can be inserted into a neural network. The image from the very start is too large to directly compress with one simple operation. It requires repetitive steps of shrinking the image by representing the features with numbers and decreasing the number of feature numbers by adding them up. These steps are repeated until the entire image that was input into the algorithm is represented by a large array of single numbers.

While this explanation might seem either very simple or difficult for some to understand, this is only a light overview of what actually happens inside the convolutional phase of the network. The process that we have just gone over is made up of many different steps that are all reliant on each other to produce the final compressed array of integers that is ready to be put into the neural network.

The first step is the convolution phase. The full image exists unchanged, and our algorithm begins to dissect the image. In the convolution phase, the image is separated into grid-like pieces, separated into smaller sections that are broken off the regular image. These grid-like sections can be defined by a certain width and height for how many rows and columns of sections you would like for the grid to be tall and wide. Depending on the size of the grid, the different sections of the grid will then be given values depending on the features present in the section. One of the most common features for a section to be identified is the color. Spots of the image, for example, that have a certain RGB value for green will be identified by this value. For other core colors in the image, such as red and blue, there will need to be separate convolutional processes for them specifically. The image otherwise would not be compressed enough with all three-color channels being identified for each segment of the grid to be able to be compressed into the grid array of integers that are required to run the image through the neural network. When the convolution step is complete, there should be a grid of values with the values identifying the amount of color for each of the core colors in the image in each section in all the grids that were extracted from the main image.

After the convolution step, we would move on to the step of max pooling. In this step, the grid from the last step with the values of the colors within each of the sections will be further compressed into a smaller grid of values. The values from a group of sections of the grid will be grouped based on the largest value in the group into a smaller grid. Just like how the regular image was broken up equally into different smaller parts which became the grids in the convolutional step, the parts of the larger sum of sections (such as the full image in the first step or the grid in this step) need to have enough sections in the image after parts of the image are already broken up to be used for compression of the data.

When we are performing the max pooling step, the grid will be usually about a fourth of the size of the last dimension, but it also depends on the method of max pooling that is being used. Max pooling can be substituted with average pooling, another method for performing the max pooling operation on the grid. The only difference with average pooling is that instead of the max number taken from a group of sections on the grid, the average number of all of the integers in a group of sections in the grid is taken and placed into a new grid.

A function that includes negative values can be optimal when a larger array of classes is needed for output, such as in situations where a negative probability makes sense. Otherwise, a function with positive values would remove the chance of error from the result of the model. This step will be repeated as many times as needed to remove abstraction from the data values and prepare them for full compression in the next stage.

In the next stage, all of the values from all of the color channels from the convolution stage will be arranged into a giant array for expressing the representation of the full image from the convolution. This stage will mark the end of the convolution-specific part of the neural network. From here on, the analysis will take place from the predictions the neural network will make about the data pieces. The ANN will take the input of the data from the convolutional stage of the model and will process them through the layers of the ANN in the same way that any pieces of data would be run through it. The output of the neural network will be the conclusion for the task the network made about the specific image. If you have made the network for classification, for example, this would be the textual name and the probability of the class the image belongs to.

The ANN would not have any substantial differences except for the shape of the input. Instead of the input being a typical piece of data, the input would consist of a vector with a large value for the representation of all of the integers from the flattening layer of the convolution stage. The ANN in this model may also have less layers than the average ANN used for a prediction or classification task alone. The fully connected layer has already done most of the compression for the ANN model, so layers without an activation function, such as shaping layers, may be reduced.

The convolution process will be used for every image in the dataset, and just as in the ANN, a full metric of accuracy will be provided at the end of the training, which can be visualized and further analyzed using visualization tools. CNN models, with all their power, may be hailed as being one of the most important advances in deep learning, but it isn't the most important. Models like ChatGPT deal with textual processing and generation. Whenever you provide it with a query, it will first use an ANN-type deep learning model to identify the knowledge it needs to utilize to craft every single part of the answer.

The model cannot just be run to create the answer all at once because all of the query at once being inserted into the model used is going to provide more noise that the model will need to preprocess using the NLP tactics we have discussed in previous chapters to craft it. It would be easier for the query of the user to be run in segments through the deep learning model, but for the model to remember the insights, it has gained from the last piece of text of the users query that has been run through the model, so it can shape the new text to be generated for the continuation of the response. This would explain why ChatGPT can begin the answer to a new user query based on the answer to a question the user has entered for the last question.

An ANN model does not have the capability to remember the value weights from the last piece of data that has run through it for the next one. The CNN model, which is based on the ANN model, also alone does not have this capability either. A model that would be able to have this capability would be based on time series forecasting. The process that this model would be based on is time series forecasting. Time series forecasting is basically the process of remembering the weights of the model for the data that has been processed through it before and using it to process data that will be processed through the model in the next intervals.

If it is possible to modify an ANN to do this, then there can be numerous possibilities for incredibly important AI applications that can be created from this, like an algorithm to generate captions for a video if paired with a CNN or an ANN to predict stock market prices. So is it possible?

The Base of ChatGPT

The answer to the question we left off with is yes. A modified ANN called an RNN has provided the skeleton model for the ChatGPT algorithm to be built on. An RNN is a type of time series forecasting model that has been popularized for providing a unique capability of AI that hasn't been possible for decades. RNNs have been the base for numerous chatbots in addition to ChatGPT and any kind of language translation software. An RNN is a type of ANN that has different kinds of layers, which are referred to in many programming languages as RNN layers and, in a version of an RNN, a time series forecasting layer.

RNNs alone do not have the capability to process image data, but if paired with a CNN, they can produce marvelous capabilities when deciphering images and providing textual output related to the image. In any applications that an ANN can be added to, an RNN can be added to provide the capabilities of time series forecasting. As we have already discussed, the capabilities of an RNN can be applied to any task that can include time series forecasting or processing data in many chunks. When paired with a CNN, the capabilities for image processing can range from image labeling to speech recognition (if the images provided are images of audio waves).

To achieve an RNN architecture, an ANN is modified to include time series forecasting, LSTM, or RNN layers. The RNN architecture includes all the features of an ANN except for the uniquely specified layers that store a gradient, which is responsible for modifying the weights of the layers and pushing them back to past layers in the network. This way, data put into the model and processed in segments can be treated in the same way as data in the past layers, but there is a problem. The gradient needs to contribute its value to the weights of each of the layers in the model to allow all of the weights to have details for processing the incoming data, which depreciates the value of the gradient for every weight it adds. This leads the gradient to have almost no effect on the data in the furthest back layers.

So what can we do to fix this? We can simply add more mechanisms for memory retention. What if instead of having only one specific channel in our RNN, we have three? These three channels will have different purposes to prevent the buildup and loss of the data. In the model, these three channels will be accessed by a layer through "gates" for moving pieces of data through the model after applying an activation function to them.

The first gate allows a layer to capture the weight and use it as a gradient that is backpropagated through the model to earlier layers. The second gate is the forget gate, which is used for deleting the gradient once it has fully passed through all of the layers of the neural network. The third gate allows the model to apply the gradient to a layer of the neural network. Every single layer in the model has an output layer, but only the last layer of the model has the input gate, and the first layer of the model has the forget gate. These different gates help to control the movement of the gradient throughout the model by having methods for deleting the gradient, applying an activation function to it when it is applied to weight from the channel, and allowing it to be backpropagated at a specific layer through the model.

Meanwhile, the input data is not being affected at all by any of these layers, which are added to the architecture to create this model. These types of networks, due to their gated structure, are not feedforward networks. ANNs are types of neural networks called feedforward since they don't have the ability to propagate or push insights through the network to the weights of past layers, whereas networks like LSTMs aren't.

In addition to the LSTM being a flavor of the RNN architecture, there is another version of an RNN model called a GRU or Gated Recurrent Unit. This neural network, just like the LSTM, has a gated structure but instead of having three gates, it has two gates.

The first gate is used for forgetting the information, and the second gate is used for updating the weights.

LSTM models may seem perfect on the outside, but they carry as many or more problems than some other deep learning models. The complexity of LSTMs and GRUs only help to add to the difficulties that the model may create. To begin, it is common sense that anything that is more difficult to understand is more difficult to fix when a problem emerges. LSTMs and GRUs contain many parts, including the gates that influence how they behave together, and if one of these parts isn't working correctly, none of them can. This is why it is best, when using an RNN network, to add as few model-specific layers as possible.

Each of these layers takes up more computational energy to run and would have a very specifically shaped input that is required for the model to work. Regular layers of a neural network usually do not require intricate shaping of the data in terms of the data's number of columns, rows, and dimensions, but RNN-based layers are picky about this metric due to the difficulties of the gating mechanisms. In addition to the difficulty of debugging, the complexity also brings the problem of the time required to train the model. Remember that everything we have mentioned about the two channels of data, the gradient, and the data the model is being trained on itself, are, in the simplest terms, mathematical operations that need to be executed by the CPU and GPU if one is available.

The more processes the model has, the more calculations the CPU and GPU need to execute to run the model. This increases the amount of time it takes for the processors to compute all of the inputs and outputs for the data. All RNN networks, as we can see, are no easy system and require distinct time for debugging and optimizing (making the model quicker). The different gates, channels, activation functions, and reshaping of the inputs require much more time than the convolutional process in a CNN or the simple application of optimizing the weights in a simple ANN. All this goes back to the theory that there is always a tradeoff between accuracy and time.

An RNN would be able to execute much faster due to the absence of the gates and a secondary channel, but it would be less accurate than an LSTM and GRU, which have them. The average running time of an LSTM model is around thirty to forty-five minutes on a device with thirty-two gigabytes of RAM. Nevertheless, while any of these models may never be able to run as fast as an ANN or CNN, they can be optimized to do so.

Recurrent Optimization

With complex models such as RNNs, it is important to decrease the amount of running time that the model may take. Even with a CNN model, a dataset that is one gigabyte large will take much more time than an LSTM running on a dataset that is twelve megabytes large. The most prominent factors in any deep learning model we have learned about so far are the units, the learning rate, and the epochs.

The learning rate is responsible for how fast the model can learn. This metric can tweak the process of gradient descent by allowing the model to learn to make the weights change by larger values to find the optimal value for them faster than they normally would. This can save time for the model to run since it will have to spend less time trying to make the weights as good of a value as they can be. The downside to using this method, though, is the chance that the model may overfit if the learning rate is too high. The most optimal amount to increase a model's learning rate is about one-fifth of its value.

The next way to optimize a model is by using the units. We have learned that units are the number of weights that each layer may have. By decreasing the amount of weights that each layer would have, we would decrease the amount of time it would take for these weights to be changed through backpropagation for each layer for each piece of data that moves through the neural network.

For RNN-based models, though, the number of units cannot be set to a very low level due to the nature of how the RNN applies the gradients for changing the weights based on data that went through the model before another set of it. This would lower the ability for the patterns or insights to be captured from the first pieces of data run through the model. The number of units may also decrease the accuracy of the results if it is decreased for a very large dataset for a similar reason. The larger the dataset is, the more features it would usually have, which would require more weights to be able to record them.

So if we want to decrease the running time of an RNN-based model or a model being trained on a big dataset, we may want to stick with changing the learning rate and the number of epochs. Changing the number of epochs can easily be done to any model no matter what kind it is or what kind of data is being processed through it. The epochs are the number of times the model will back-propagate the gradient through it to change the weights during the training process. The fewer epochs there are, the less time the model will need to do this, which will save time.

Any of these methods, when applied to any model, can help to decrease the run time by quite a bit.

How Are Different Types of Software Built on Top of RNNs

As we have learned by now, RNN models have amazing capabilities. While they do have a complex structure, they can produce remarkable results and create innovative predictions based on past sequences of data. So how would an RNN be used for language translation software?

Well, apart from the GUI, or graphical user interface, where the user types in the query for the model to process, you first would need to collect data online about a base language that you would like the user to start out with, such as English, and a secondary language to which they would translate, such as French. The model would take as input a CSV file full of rows of a word in English and a translation of the word in French.

As we know, before running the model on these words, we need to use NLP methods to remove abstraction from the text and make it more friendly for processing by the computer. The text would then be shaped to the appropriate number of columns to fit into the RNN model. The model would then take the training text in different chunks and begin learning the structure of the data from the English language data by adjusting the weights of the model, and it would begin matching the phrases in English to those in French.

A piece of data would enter the model, and the data within the word would be processed through each of the neurons in a layer using the $w + mx = b$ equation, and then this result would fit into the activation function of a neuron. A gradient would then be formed from the neuron, and it would be pushed through the input gate into the gradient channel, which will modify the weights of all of the neurons before it. For the last layer, it will contain an output layer. This will be added to the result of the main channel, where our word in English will be multiplied by the gradient. When the model is then fully trained, you will be able to predict a result from an individual piece of data from the set. For the aggregation of these values for all the words in the training data, we will receive the accuracy for the model. You can also try a phrase from the English dictionary that was not present in the dataset, but this may give a less accurate result than a phrase the model was trained on.

RNN models with their gated structure have also paved the way for more gated and complex deep learning models, which can extend from different, more advanced versions of the RNN and other models with a different architecture that produce the same result as the RNN. For simplicity, we will just focus on these models. RNNs can be used in just about any application that has to do with generating, analyzing, or translating text, which makes it a logical base for an advanced chatbot such as ChatGPT. ANN, CNN, and RNN models are the very basis that any more complicated model is built on within the deep learning environment. Some models may tweak the architecture of one of the models, but they will always be based on the theory of the ANN with convolution or time series forecasting or both.

Deep learning has different models made for different applications such as image analysis (CNN), text generation (RNN), and general analysis tasks on simple datasets (ANN). But what about creating images from scratch? One of the most prominent capabilities of ChatGPT is to be able to create any image from scratch from a simple query the user may enter in. If we also want to complete our goal of understanding whether or not AI can be hailed as being safe and whether it is worth developing further, we need to touch on one of its most powerful and expansive features.

Text generation is very important, but one of the most prominent ways to convey any message is through an image. It only makes sense that if we want to know the dangers of AI and how they can be prevented, we would talk about one of the most misused features of AI, which can create the most destruction: image generation.

Image generation is a newer part of AI compared to the other fields we have discussed. Image generation is also more difficult to achieve than other tasks in AI due to the complexity of creation. There are many different questions that image generation can pose for certain types of data, such as very high-quality images you may want to generate, such as 4K photographs, or images with a certain style, such as anime or minimalistic. To be able to create these kinds of images, wouldn't you need to tweak the model every time you want to create an image that the model has not been trained on in a new style? Also, how would the actual creation of the colored pixels in an array to be represented as an image even take place? Don't images contain billions or even trillions of pixels?

These are questions that computer scientists have been grappling with for years, and we are lucky enough to live during a time when we have easy access to their solutions from anywhere in the world through books and the Internet. For reasons of complexity, image generation has taken much longer to develop than other forms of machine learning and deep learning. Many researchers have also needed to build upon older models to create models such as those used for image generation.

Image generation might be very complex, but in the world of computer science, it is possible to make the impossible possible through the power of logic and imagination. So let's see how methods for image generation have been made a reality.

An Interesting Picture

A very well-known phrase for millennia is that a picture is worth a thousand words. This is just as true in the past as it is today. If anyone had an option between looking at a piece of text to describe an event in a newspaper or looking at a picture, they would almost certainly choose the picture. Humans have always been able to conceive more information about any event or object from a picture than from a piece of text when asked to describe it. Humans have a natural tendency to use their sight of vision to be able to perceive something in as much detail as they can so it would only make sense that a technology that can change the way we think about computing would be able to create content that allows us to use AI to generate images.

Using inspiration from the ANN architecture and the CNN architecture, researchers have been able to create a model to generate images in a very unlikely way with a very unlikely name. Generative adversarial networks, also called GANs, are models that researchers have created to generate images from a bunch of random noise or data in an image, which doesn't look like anything at the beginning, to look similar to images within the training set of data. But what is this random data? How does the image over time come to look like the image in the training set, and why exactly does the name have the word *adversary* in it? These are all questions that can explain the inner workings of image recognition.

Image generation is a very different task from text generation, image analysis, and general prediction and classification using deep learning. Image generation is a much more complex process, in which the process of text generation can outpace its speed by about four times. It is a very long and computationally heavy process that can produce remarkable results. Image generation is another generative process, just like text generation done by LSTMs or GRUs, but it is done in a much different way. GANs also do not have a gated structure, including a separate channel for the gradient to be added to the weights, meaning that GANs can also suffer from a disappearing gradient just like models such as the RNN but to a lesser extent.

Images cannot be generated in chunks where knowledge of the features of one image needs to be fed to the weights of the other neurons in the network to avoid missing data, so it would be unnecessary to overcomplicate an already complicated process to be able to achieve the ability to perform a task that is not even necessary. Therefore, many functionalities which did unfortunately lead to some problems down the line have been removed from the GAN to be able to achieve the simplest method to perform a complicated process.

GAN models are deep learning models, which means that they are based on the underlying architecture of the ANN, but they have some differences. Unlike models that we have seen earlier, there are two parts of this one that work together to make the process possible: the generator and the discriminator. The generator is the part of the model that is responsible for creating the images, and the discriminator is responsible for figuring out which images are part of the training dataset and which are made by the generator. Those made by the generator are scored by the discriminator on how closely they look to those from the training set, and depending on this score, the weights in the generator are adjusted to produce more similar-looking images to those in the training set.

Over time, the generator will achieve a more optimal result for the images, and the discriminator will change the weight less in the generator, similar to the weights in a neural network. The generator consists of the same layers that can be found in any neural network but in larger quantities with the inclusion of reshaping layers to process the output of the shape into the right input for the discriminator. Unlike other models we have talked about, the GAN also does not have any model-specific layers in the basic models. It doesn't seem very difficult, right? Well, this isn't all. It's the way in which the discriminator and generator are used that makes this model complex.

We now know about the neural networks and the main parts of the model, but what about the input? The GAN model has two main parts, so the process of training it will also be in two steps, with each step for each part. The generator requires some kind of frame to generate the images over. This input would come in the form of half a batch of images included in the training set. With these images, we would create noise or distortions to the data to make a clean base for the generator to use for constructing the images. Images in this form would look similar to a cable TV screen when the signal is lost and creating static. The tiny bits of distorted color are what the generator is going to modify over time to create the full image. So let's see it in action.

Image Generation in Action

Let's say we would like to generate an image based on a user query about a specific animal. For simplistic purposes, this animal will either need to be a cat, dog, horse, cow, sheep, mouse, tiger, or wolf. Depending on the amount of images in the dataset, we would define the epochs the model should be trained on as this number. To create an image with as high quality as possible, we need to confine the options for generation to the classes in the dataset that our GAN was trained on.

So let's begin the training process. The first thing we need to do is resize the images to be able to fit into the layers of the GAN. This would be done using a resize layer that we mentioned before. Next, we would initialize (create) the set of commands that will be responsible for creating the generator. Then we create an input layer to hold one of the dimensions of the input data, which would be named the latent dimension. Then we would recreate the generator using this layer. The next thing we would do is set the ability of the generator to be trained to false. We do this to prevent the generator from overfitting the data.

After this, we would set the random noise in the form of ones and zeros for the generator to create the image over. The generator for every image it processes from the training images, the generator would generate based on the sequences of RGB values in them by adjusting the values in the array of random noise. Then we would train the discriminator over the half batch of training set images and the images the generator had created out of the random noise that we have defined as the frame for the generator to create the old images over. These images can be viewed as progressing into its true form interval by interval through different data visualization techniques, but we will just be focusing on the model.

The discriminator would then assign a score to each image by comparing the arrangements and colors of the pixel values from the generator images to those of the training images. The process will then start over again, and the generator will have its weights modified depending on this value. This process will repeat over and over again until the amount of epochs has been reached.

GANs present a hallmark in the development of artificial intelligence, a step forward in the field of advanced pattern recognition and generative AI. GANs are actually an even bigger step forward in the field than NLP or RNNs. GANs possess the true capabilities of generative AI with their ability to create meaning out of random noise and match the data in the training set with it. Generative AI may have first started with RNNs, but the architecture to pave the way forward is the GAN model.

GANs have been one of the only models to be a breakthrough in the field of deep learning and probability together. Deep learning models have made very little to do with random activity apart from the modifying of the weights. The ability for the GAN to be able to create random noise which the neural network can use to modify the appearance of the image is where probability and deep learning meet together.

The Downfall of GANs

While there are numerous things that the GAN outweighs other models by, just like with every model in the field of AI, there is always a tradeoff between the accuracy of the model and the speed computationally of the model to be able to produce these results.

With their immense power, GANs, unfortunately, are the slowest deep learning models to date, even with the minimum amount of data they are set to train on. The architecture of the GAN sets it up to take a very long time to run due to the need for the discriminator and the generator to each be trained on different sets of data and their need to communicate with each other. The generation process itself is also time-consuming in computational terms.

While many of the processes of computers may be viewed as being performed at light speed, more complex processes can be visually longer. This is why researchers created the method of stochastic gradient descent in the first place. Computers are not superhuman objects. They can perform any logical task quicker than humans can, but they cannot perform any task this way, just as computationally demanding tasks. Images can have millions of tiny pixels that make them up, depending on the resolution. Images with higher resolution have more pixels, resulting in a clearer image, but lower resolution images have fewer pixels. This makes the creation of higher-resolution images lengthier in time.

GANs also have difficulties when it comes to datasets with an unequal amount of images from different classes or groupings. When a GAN model is given a query to create a certain kind of image that the model has had less training on, it will produce this image in a much worse way than an image from another class. So it is important to have a dataset with an equal number of images in every class. GAN models, like any AI model, will learn what and however they are programmed to learn, following and perceiving data the way they are trained, just like any baby is taught to see the world and behave.

A far more serious issue with GANs, which can have a substantial impact on their accuracy, is the loss of certain features in the images they create. In an image, there will always be objects of different sizes and shapes and of different colors. Depending on these characteristics, the model may ignore or poorly represent one of these objects in a poorer way than the others. This can be seen in some images generated by AI, such as fingers on a hand being either too many, improperly placed, or improperly shaped. This is one of the features of AI that still requires further improvement.

GANs are very comparable models in the complex tasks they can perform almost effortlessly, but they are not the only ones. GANs have set the stage for other models based on their unique generative architecture to arise, such as video generation models. Since videos are just a bundle of image frames separated from each other by very short intervals of time, they can be easily recreated using the techniques from the GAN model for image creation done many times for the recreation of one video. Some new developments in AI even allow users to create animated images based on images they feed the model based on a certain prompt.

We have now seen almost everything in the realm of basic AI. From the simple models of naive Bayes to predict the probability of an event to text generation using LSTMs, we have seen almost all of what AI can do to replicate human activities and perform wondrous computational tasks. As many of the models appear, they raise many questions about their capabilities to be used for harm and for good. If a model that is based on our own brains is misused, how far can it go wrong? Will we ever see an AI that can become our own adversary? Should we begin now to restrict AI's capabilities and reach? With a solid understanding of AI, we now have the capability to answer these questions.

The first part of this book focused on the different sections of AI, such as machine learning, deep learning, and NLP. We looked at many of the main models in each of these fields, what they can be used for, how they work, their cons, and an example problem being solved using one of these models. But now it is time to answer the big question: How does AI impact society?

With a solid understanding of both the technological and algorithmic ends, we can look at how AI will influence our everyday lives and other parts of society that we may not come into direct contact with but are still important. This begins with the corporate side, the personal side, the international side, and the social side. By looking at all of these sides, we will gain an understanding of how AI impacts these systems and what can be done about it. Some impacts may be positive, and others may not be, so we need to see both sides of each of the situations to be able to understand what will be the full impact of AI. But first we will need an introduction for when was AI beginning to be used in society.

As you can see, the method is very straightforward for a task such as this. The same methods can be applied to any dataset, but the preprocessing stages can vary in what dataset is being processed. Different datasets may need to be processed in different ways depending on factors such as their variations.

Variations of Models

This process can also be modified depending on the specific type of GAN model being used. Just like the RNN model has many different variations, the GAN model also has different variations to suit different types of datasets, which may possess different elements of concern. One of the most prominent is the problem of the vanishing gradient. As we have seen before, models can suffer from this problem when the gradient for adjusting the weights shrinks every time it is applied to a layer in the network. Likewise, in the GAN model, the problem of the vanishing gradient can be observed in the generator when a weight assigns probabilities to generated samples matching samples in the training set. When these values are very small, to begin with, the gradient, when pushed back through the network for adjusting the weights via backpropagation, will shrink to a very small size. But with a quicker learning rate, this problem should be minimized over time. Different variations of different models in machine learning make changes to certain parameters or functions of the model.

AI and the Society Part 1: Will AI Make Creativity Obsolete?

For many years, humans have worried about AI making creativity obsolete. People believed that AI, with the ability to mimic our own brains, would eventually outperform us in many different facets of life, including in creative works. The art of creativity entails primarily taking experiences or different elements and connecting them together to create something new. Some instances of this can be logical, like coming up with the solution to a tough problem, and others can be aesthetic, such as a new idea for a picture you would like to draw to portray the message of a certain event or message you would like other people to know about. Think about any image that comes to mind—what would it be made of? Vincent van Gogh's famous image of *The Starry Night* comprises a long shrub in front of a beautiful mountain village under a beautiful night sky. Would it be possible for AI to fully replicate this?

In the past, it was very unlikely for this to happen, but with new developments in AI technology such as the GAN, the increase of computational power with more powerful CPUs coming out, and general big steps in the field of AI research becoming present, this has started to seem plausible. The biggest leap, though, was with the unveiling of Midjourney, a very famous generative AI model that can generate images from a query that a user can type in. Midjourney is basically a version of a very advanced GAN model combined with an LSTM model for being able to make understanding out of text to allow the model to be able to creat images from it. The model was also trained on a very diverse dataset of images to be truly generative. You can ask Midjourney to create an image in almost any aesthetic, and it will generate a finely crafted image that can be almost indistinguishable from a human artist's work.

This means that the model would need to have been trained on data that was scraped (collected) from different websites around the Internet without asking permission for the use of these images. This is one of the first problems of generative AI. There has been a big scandal ever since the creation of generative AI over the rights of what images AI can be trained on. Some artists may have posted their works on websites that the AI algorithm may use for data collection for training the model. This would not only be an impeding issue on privacy but also to the creative works of others.

As we have seen before, art is defined as the combination of different thoughts, events, and objects to represent a message. In the case of Midjourney, the message is what the user would type into the query box on the website of the Midjourney model. The thoughts, or the parts of the model, would also be someone else's, collected without their permission, not only an infringement of privacy but also of their rights to their work, being used to create an artwork for someone who has not given any recognition for the work of the artist that is being used.

The algorithms that scrape the data from different websites usually do not acknowledge who the artist is, what the website is, or whether the artist allows free use of their image or not. The algorithms to scrape the data are just as smart as the computer itself: smart enough to only do what someone programs them to do. The algorithm is not going to collect data because it wants to steal someone else's work; it is only doing it because someone wrote the code to allow it to do so. Scraping algorithms usually run over as many sites on the Internet as possible to collect data, especially for data-demanding generative AI models.

Luckily, web developers know about these types of programs beforehand and create certain access requirements for websites, such as the confirm-you-are-not-a-robot task, which usually contains a box that you need to check or another task that you need to perform to confirm that you are human. However, due to the excessive dislike of these checks people to have to deal with these checks and for other circumstances, developers will simply block any kind of scraping software from entering their sites. Unfortunately, AI has now become intelligent enough to bypass these barriers or enter sites where they simply don't have any barriers or checkpoints. Just Google "ChatGPT solves CAPTCHA" to see many instances where this happens. So there isn't anything that can fully stop AI from going onto websites and scraping up information that it may not be allowed to do in the first place. So is there anything that can be done?

The Legal Battle of AI vs Creators

Many artists rely on reparations for their work to make compensation for their hard work, and if this is being overhauled, what have they done? Some artists have sued companies creating generative AI art creating algorithims over the misuse of their work in images that they are creating. Some images that AI makes can even visually show the watermark of an artist, proving that their work is being used in the creation of images by the model.

Lawmakers at the local, state, and national levels are still discussing what can be done about intellectual property being scraped off the Internet and used by bots. Artists, on their end, state that the use of their work in training AI models should be against the law for intellectual property protection, but AI companies, on the other hand, state that because the AI model has made the artwork, the AI model should hold full rights to the artwork, not the artists.

But should the model really have any rights to the artwork? AI models, as we have learned, are simply algorithms that mimic the human brain through our way of learning. AI models do not receive compensation for what they make, nor do they even know what they are creating. AI models do not even know what money is until you actively tell them what it is.

Artists, on the other hand, spend hours or days instead of milliseconds creating their work, and some may even do this for a living. If they do not earn compensation for what they are creating, then they are being unfairly screwed by a brand-new technology that still does not have many rules in its way. Artists are humans, and humans should be acknowledged for their creative work. More laws need to be developed around how AI can and cannot be trained and used.

As a new technology, it may not be very well understood, and people may still be convinced that they can wait longer until they need to do something about it, but it will become clearer as time progresses that this issue needs action right now.

What Can Be Done to Solve This Problem?

One thing that can be done to help bring more attention to this issue is for artists to continue placing watermarks on their images. Watermarks are a kind of signature on digital images that state the artist's name. These watermarks are not removed from the image during the process of the image being reshaped to fit into a GAN model. The water mark also as being a central part of the image cannot also be removed or hidden either by modifying color channels in the image, tweaking the effects applied to the image such as blurriness, rotation, or translation.

If a watermark were to be attempted to be removed from the image, the part of the image where the watermark once sat would appear distorted compared to the rest of the image. As we already know, images have many different features or objects inside of them, and some features are more prominent than others. A signature with high contrast to its surrounding features in the image would be easily identifiable and would remain during the entire data preprocessing and throughout its journey inside the deep learning model, represented as an array of bits. This method can be a great way for artists to allow their work to be identified if it is possibly trained on a generative AI image creation model.

Some other methods artists can use to prevent their images ending up in training data is putting their images on certain websites that are known to be far less popular so there is a less likely chance that a scraping algorithm used to train a generative AI model will come across it, or for artists to put accessing their images behind paywalls on more popular websites.

What Can Companies Do To Solve This Problem?

Companies behind models like Midjourney try to respect the rights of artists for their work and do not want to create models that can potentially be harmful to other people's rights. The entire algorithms which they build are not the culprits for this problem. The scraping algorithms, which are the reason why the work of artists is even ending up in AI models in the first place, are the main culprits. So why not put restrictions on them?

Scraping algorithms themselves cannot choose what websites they go to; they simply go to whatever websites they have been programmed to go to. If they are programmed to go to any website they want to go to, then they will do exactly that. Developers, however, can define what websites they want the scrapers not to go to by using constraints. For example, a developer can program a web scraping algorithm to avoid websites of a certain type, such as a video-sharing platform like YouTube. Likewise, a developer can restrict scraping software to go to smaller sites that contain content from a certain kind of field.

Developers can also use AI to scan images for watermarks in the data preprocessing phase of the model to identify images created by artists. If such an image is identified, it can be removed from the dataset the model is being trained on.

However, even with the proper utilization of these solutions, it is still important for lawmakers and those in positions of power to know the dangers of AI and intellectual property rights. Artists alone can only do so much to demand proper treatment of their work. AI may seem like a black box to an outsider, but it is an important algorithm that can be understood with the study of its theory and more awareness raised for it. Creativity in its purest form can only be human, but at a more abstract level, it can be done by both humans and AI.

Creativity at a Deeper Level

How should we exactly define creativity for AI compared to humans? Human creativity is the ability to connect many different events, objects, or thoughts together to make something completely new. But what is it for AI? AI, in many ways, can do things that include some form of creativity, such as using probability. Creativity in humans is based on the purely random events of different thoughts in our heads connecting. Randomness in the field of computing is not based on purely random events. Instead, randomness in computer science is factored around a certain amount of randomness with some known patterns.

For example, in this list: 2, 4, 6, 7, if I were to ask the computer to pick a random number from it, I might, for the first five times, get a sequence of numbers where no number repeated once. But after the fifth time, I might begin to see the number 7 repeating in the sequence of numbers every third time. Is this an accident? If it happens enough times, it wouldn't be. Computers are incapable of generating truly random numbers, so therefore they do have creativity that may not be noticeable to an outsider but on the interior the algorithmic process that is required to create this randomality makes the pure creativity that humans have impossible for computers until innovations in the feild are made. AI also uses randomality for many different types of tasks inside of computer vision, machine learning, and deep learning.

So we can say that AI does use an aspect of creativity like humans do in their decision-making process, although in a different way. In addition to AI's creativity being used in image generation, it is also being used in textual responses.

Creative Writing

Similar to the problems image-generating AIs have created, generative AI text models (also known as large language models or LLMs) can also infringe on privacy, but this time less directly. AI large language models can imitate the writing styles of different authors whose papers the model has been trained on. AI-generated text, as we have learned, does not come out of nowhere; LSTMs and GRUs are the main reasons for this ability.

The models need to find a large set of training data so they can understand how human language is constructed and how to make intelligent responses with all kinds of wording. Text is another way for someone to express themselves, so is anything being done about it? Unfortunately, many people are still using this to their advantage by allowing AI to effortlessly write long texts based on its given query. This can bring up very similar issues to the problems with digital art being used in the training sets of AI models.

AI with textual and image generation is a threat to most pieces of work that humans may create, but what about other intellectual property?

AI and Other Skills

As we now know, AI is becoming more and more developed by the day. There is a lot at stake for any creative freelancer who is putting their work out onto the Internet. But what about other intellectual property? The realm of intellectual property contains many more products than just pieces of art and writing. Well, AI, as of right now, cannot copy physically made goods or patent them itself, nor does it have any intention of its own to do so. Intellectual property that is not confined to digital creative work will be safe from being overtaken or used by AI.

AI's main skills to date are image generation, video generation, and text generation. Today, AI's abilities still render it inferior to practitioners from many other fields. AI has skills primarily in intellectual tasks, but physical tasks are currently very difficult for even an intelligent robot to complete. Robots have a long way to go before being able to create a physical painting that can be bought to be hung in someone's home. Therefore, creatives can be free of fear of AI copying their work as long as it is in a physical form.

Other forms of art that do not exclusively involve technology are also safer from AI domination. Fields like dance and theater cannot be overtaken by AI as long as there is no intelligent algorithm coupled with an ultra-intelligent robot trained to participate in these activities at a professional level.

But with all of this, there still may be a bright side for intellectual property. A full image of an artist cannot be entirely replicated in the exact same way the artist has made it. AI can only accurately make about half of any image. AI always creates products based on those of the input, but when creating something out of nothing other than a very basic base like the GAN model, the AI will not be able to fully recreate the same images it has been trained on. Generative AI, just like GAN models for image generation, also cannot create textual or visual responses that will be able to entirely mimic a piece of training data that may be the creation of someone else. An instance of an image being solely used to a visual extent of the output is very rare. Knowing this, about 90 percent of all artwork and stories published online are protected from any kind of direct plagiarism.

Any kind of physically created intellectual property is the safest, and the safest intellectual property online is moderately safe unless it is behind a paywall or on a very secure site that does not allow access by web scraping software.

With future developments in the physical abilities of AI, it may be wise for creators in any field to begin tagging their work in a similar way to how digital artists should tag their artwork with a watermark to clarify its authenticity against AI-generated artwork. This way, if there are any advancements within the field of AI that may allow it to replicate even physical intellectual property, creatives will be able to quickly identify their work and will be able to issue a complaint about it being used in generated content. Different ways of storing intellectual property will be one of the keys to protecting it coming along. One of the best ways to do this is simply to remove a digital presence from the product. Our digital presence is being remade by AI. The internet once was controlled solely by search engines fetching links to lead us to information from a simple search query, but today generative AI is allowing us to bypass those links, and it is feeding us the information simply by asking it. The Internet therefore is becoming much more intertwined than ever before. AI also may have the potential to render search engines obsolete.

AI and the Society Part 1: The Future of the Internet with AI

"The cloud is going to make software obsolete!" This was a common term for developers from the 2010s to 2020 when cloud computing was beginning to take off. Software for a very long time was something that was usually encoded onto a disk and fed into a device for use, but a lot has changed since then. With the introduction of the iPhone, people realized that bigger is not always better, and ever since, people have vied for smaller and more optimal things.

Software, since the dawn of personal computers, has been at the center of the world of computing. Whenever someone used a computer or a phone, they used the software on it, whether it was the operating system or the apps on it. People were tired of very big downloads that would make their devices run slower, and developers were especially tired of running machine learning applications with computers that were very slow to handle the load. Personal computers had to be quickly improved to handle the pressure of use people were putting on them by downloading so many applications that would bog down the hard drive of the devices or run tasks on them that would tire the CPU and RAM.

Enter newer, much more expensive enterprise-level computers that have about one hundred gigabytes more RAM than the average computer and thousands of times more storage. This was a computer that everyone could use to run their applications on but could not touch. These computers weren't connected to any kind of monitor; they were simply lone computers used for computational resources. Large tech companies found this to be a great solution to the problem of personal computers' inability to hold software. They started purchasing these devices or manufacturing them and placing them in database storage. Companies began pushing services to these storage places to allow the easy use of highly demanded computation software to improve their business. Developers also began running and creating software on these platforms by using services that these big tech companies created for using computers.

This was the birth of cloud computing. Cloud computing is a kind of strange name for this practice because real clouds are not at all involved in the process of this service, but the service itself works like one. Clouds are objects in the sky made out of condensed water. You may never get to touch one, but you still know that it is there, just like the computers used in cloud computing. This practice has become so popular that billions of people on the Internet today don't even know that they are using applications containing cloud computing when they are browsing the Internet. Cloud computing became the next step in a concept: software, which was very old and needed improvement. This same concept is what can change the Internet with AI.

The Internet is also a very old concept. The Internet may be newer than software, but it is not that much different from it. For one, the Internet is its own software. If we want to use the Internet, we need software to allow us to do this. Also, the Internet wasn't as easy to use as software was in the very beginning.

When the first personal computers came out, there were very few things you could do on them. They had one simple window that looked like and was used like MS-DOS or the shell terminal on MacBook for using the Internet. You would type in cryptic-looking commands with the URL of a website you wanted to go to online, press enter, and the terminal would take you there. There was no search bar or news on the window. Not to mention, the results were also difficult to navigate through. When you received the results, you would need to type in very similar cryptic commands with the only difference being the number of your choice instead of the URL that you wanted to navigate to. Then the terminal would take you to the website only for you to see it appear in a very ugly-looking format that was no easier to navigate than the terminal window.

Since then, Netscape has created the first graphical user interface, or GUI for short, to allow the easy navigation of the Internet that we enjoy today. They are the pioneers of the search bar and the organized links placed right underneath it after the search results are fetched. Since then, nontechnical people from around the world have become immediate Internet users. We may be seeing a similar advent coming soon with the abilities of AI.

AI also started out as something that was created primarily for researchers at academic institutions to either aid them with tasks or as a topic of further study. Faster and more powerful chips and more developed algorithms have extended the capabilities of AI far beyond this point. The abilities of text generation and image generation were the primary abilities for AI to enter into the realm of completing everyday intellectual and Internet tasks. Using this ability and its very wide database of training data, it can be a new superintelligent search engine. AI, with its new text generation capabilities, can seemingly generate humanlike text. AI also can search through its vast database of knowledge and can gather up the information that can match as closely as possible to the query of the user and present it to the user in an easier format than millions of links on the screen to search through.

Getting your specific information from the Internet directly is a big step forward. Millions of people have struggled to find what they are looking for whenever they type a query into the search box on the Internet. There can be hundreds of millions of links that contain potential information that you may need, but questions can arise: Are the sites credible? Are they safe? Do they even have the accurate response that I am looking for? All these questions have posed many barriers to the efficient use of the Internet for research.

The Internet mainly works by searching through the text on almost all the websites on the Internet at light speed and finding websites that contain keywords similar to those that you have included in your query. This method worked very well at first when websites were simple and when the use of the Internet for highly complex tasks was still very light, but today it is very different. Today, people are searching for more and more specific things.

There is a big difference in the accuracy of the search results that may come up in a search for "What was the weather last Friday in Seattle, Washington?" and "How many hours was it raining last Friday in Seattle, Washington?" The first result will bring up more accurate answers than the latter result. For the first result, the Internet search engine, depending on the type you are using, will search through the sites by first looking for the keywords *weather* and *Seattle* together. Then on pages that it finds, it will narrow down the results to pages containing the keywords *last* and *Friday*. This will give you the most accurate results of the two queries (with only a few miscellaneous sites brought in).

On the other hand, for the second option, there are many more keywords that the algorithm needs to factor in. The newer words *Friday* and *rain* filter out many more results and create a much tighter specification for the browser to fulfill when filtering out links for results. With the decreased ability to do very specific searches on their browsers, people have lost hope in being able to successfully use modern browsers.

With the introduction of generative AI, this is all going to change. ChatGPT and Google's Bard have the ability to search through a giant corpus of all data available to us on the Internet without us even needing to see it at nearly fifty times the speed. All we see is the end result of the answer that we are looking for in a very human-friendly readable form. Most people who perform searches online are not searching for specific websites but rather for information from those websites.

For example, someone who may be logging in to their PayPal account on the PayPal website is using the Internet to access a certain website, whereas someone who makes a search online to figure out the best methods to design a modern, minimalistic website is explicitly searching for information. The person who is searching for how to design their website, unlike the first person who can quickly tap the first result they find in the results and complete their desired task, needs to search through possibly hundreds of results to find the full answer or parts of the answer on how to build their website.

This can be incredibly time-consuming depending on what the purpose is for doing this. If someone needs help to complete a plan for a website launch, then figuring out how to make the website look very modern and minimalistic is only one of the first tasks that need to be completed. What about SEO (search engine optimization) for the site? What about actually coding up the website and hosting it?

To be able to learn how to do all these things, if you do not already know how, you will need to spend excessive time just searching the Internet for trustworthy results. On top of all of this, for search engines to make money, they even allow sites that can be remotely related to the search that you are trying to make to be pushed to the top of the search results. These are sites that pay for the ability for their site to pop up based on a certain word in the search.

This can cause even more frustration for the user when they are trying to find what they are looking for. They not only have to deal with sites that may not be trustworthy and sites that may be phishing but also sites that are simply advertisements that have very little to do with what the user has actually searched for. All these irrelevant sites together piled up on top of the other results that can actually contain information to aid the user's search, make it unbelievably difficult to find the information you are looking for in a timely manner.

Depending on what your job may be, this time can be costly. If you, for example, are a developer who is searching online for methods to solve the bug you are facing, the more time you spend searching online, the slower the delivery time is for the software you are trying to create. The slower your team will also be able to work as a whole when you are being consumed with fixing one problem for a long period of time. This leads entire departments and even companies of development teams to deliver slower and buggier software that makes the user experience much more unpleasant and drives away users from the company's product. This is only because it took too long for a developer to fix a bug in their code due to all the irrelevant search results they were receiving online for the problem they were facing.

Many industries currently face this problem, and this leads to problems getting fixed visually slower than with a timely ability to be able to solve problems. When all this is added up together, the society as a result begins to be less eficeient. Everyone after all who uses the internet relies on it being their top resoruce to go to when seraching up a specific issue. No book, newspaper, or document in history has and will ever contain as much information as the Internet does today. It only makes sense that in a time when innovation takes center stage, we should be able to overcome such a difficulty.

Enter generative AI. ChatGPT, Google's Bard, and other large language models have provided a much-needed feature that the Internet was lacking. We can swiftly type in what we want to know, and we get a simple explanation brought to us in an easy way. Using this technology, we can sift through millions of links on the Internet in milliseconds. This makes the Internet much more usable and fast, but can this be entirely the new Internet?

Will, in the future, instead of needing to type what we want in a Google or Bing search bar to get our desired result and then click on a link to access it, we just receive a clear explanation from a large language model that is employed by the browser? Well, yes and no. The Internet is used for many things, and as we have seen before, people use the Internet for many more things than simply searching for the answers to questions they don't know yet.

This kind of method for a start will not allow the basic ability to access a specific website like Amazon simply to do shopping on it. An LLM will simply output an explanation of the company of Amazon or what the Amazon site is instead of taking us to the actual site. The Internet has certainly evolved over the decades, but we will need major changes to be made before we are able to go to any site on the web without clicking a link. Links have been the backbone of the Internet. They are the main way to identify any site that exists on the Internet, so what would happen if we didn't use them anymore? Can the Internet really continue to exist?

A simple structure like links, to be replaced or used in a completely different way, will have to be a major change to a system that is already very complex. Allowing an AI to automatically click a link for us when we ask it to take us to a certain site can be a major point of debate. On one hand, online safety is at stake. What if the AI makes a mistake and takes us to a website we would have never originally intended to go to? This website could possibly contain viruses for our device, may have unsafe content on it, or try to scam us. What if the creators of these systems could also possibly hack into large language models that are bound to take us directly to the site we please to make them take us to their sites for common search queries that we might feed into the AI? These are all important ramifications to consider before we let AI take the main wheel, which can promote further discussion on how safe it would be to let AI do much more important things without our direct guidance.

Internet search has recently become so widely used and so complex that it may not be wise to let something such as AI take the driver's wheel. Generative AI, after all, is still in its first stages of development. We need to allow it more time for development and research before we can let it do tasks of larger and larger importance for us. The Internet from the very beginning was made to be decentralized, just like the blockchain. This means that no entity has full control over it. This is what has allowed the Internet to grow so big over time and so much miscellaneous content to end up on it. This is why we need to allow AI to become more developed and teach it more about the Internet, along with putting tighter restrictions on it, before we can let it be our main eyes on the Internet. So how can we use AI right now for better Internet search while remaining safe on the Internet? Well, to begin with, why not use it for giving us the answers to the most complex queries we may search for?

The Power of AI for Filtering

We already know that very specific queries can stump the regular search browser by giving us unconventional results, so why not give this filtering process to AI? AI can perform much faster and more powerful filtering for very chunky queries so why not we use it for one of its best abilities? If we want to search for a very specific fact that we don't want to spend hours in the library or on Wikipedia searching for, why not use AI to give us exactly what we need?

AI can, within milliseconds, filter out results from all the sites that exist across the Internet, no matter how specific the query may be. If the query also may be factually incorrect or it may be entirely false, AI can also give us an indication of this too before searching through all the incorrect results online to be able to find this out later. This surely can be a helpful tool also when trying to fact-check certain facts in feilds that you may have very little knowlege in also. This brings us to the next best way to use AI for Internet search.

The Power of AI for Learning

Just like the ability of AI to perform fact-checking on things we may not know, we can also use AI to learn complex facts. Large language models are notorious for their simplified way of explaining information to us in a human-friendly context. If we want to learn about something that is either very difficult to find information about on the Internet or is just very difficult to find a simple explanation for, AI is the go-to option for being able to have a private tutor free of any cost for teaching us a skill.

AI can give very detailed but easy-to-understand explanations for anything we want to learn. It can also give us the information in any way we would like it to. For example, if we may want a quick overview of the topic, we can simply ask the AI to give this to us. If we would like a detailed description of one section of the topic that we want to find information about online for than, we can receive this also by simply asking for AI to give it to us.

On the other hand, if you may be someone who may learn better through watching videos on the topic, then AI can give you this too. It can provide a list for the best-rated videos from all over the Internet on the topic you want to learn. AI also can take any further questions on the topic you may ask about it. For example, if after watching a video about the third unit of AP chemistry, you may have a question on organic chemistry, then you can ask AI specifically about questions that you may have relating to organic chemistry. This can allow you to thoroughly be able to study any topic you may please without needing to fill in knowledge gaps beforehand.

How You Should Not Use AI for Search

As we have already mentioned, there are many things that AI is not yet ready to do when it comes to optimizing our Internet browsing experience, such as taking us directly to the websites we may wish to go to from a simple query. However, there are other things we also must keep in mind when using AI for searching the Internet.

First, do not ask it questions in the exact same way you would ask another human being. Although AI has been trained on a lot of human-written content and generally understands the way humans communicate with each other, it is still not a good idea to do this. For one, AI can misinterpret your question because of biases it may have in the data it has been trained on. AI is only as smart as the content it is trained on. If you train even the most advanced AI on content from conspiracy theories or political propaganda websites, and if you ask it certain questions, it will output results in relation to the beliefs of the people who wrote content on those sites. Do not assume that AI is as smart as you may think it is!

Secondly, AI does not understand core human values, and it also may not understand some kinds of jokes or satire. This can lead it to producing potentially harmful, inappropriate, or worrying results when asking it a query that may pertain to specifically one of these topics.

While we may currently have the algorithm down for creating one of the most humanlike AIs that can ever exist, we do not have many other important aspects developed for it yet. So you may want to ask your best friend to react to one of the funniest jokes you just came up with before asking ChatGPT. Certain topics, such as who may be a better candidate for a political office or thoughts on ongoing conficts in the news, may also be best kept out of the realm of questions that you should ask AI.

To put it all into perspective, AI is not a human. Yes, it may write responses just like one, but it does not have our core human values nor our exact experiences and interpretations of the world. AI also is not as intelligent and developed as we may think it is, and certain ways of using it for optimizing Internet search and giving us logical standings on controversial topics are out of its reach for now.

AI should be thought of as only a more advanced search engine for helping us get better explanations about complex topics, fact-checking, and getting more convenient explanations for difficult-to-find information on the Internet and very specific queries. Next, we will look into one of the most debated questions about AI: Will AI take over our jobs? This has become an ever more important question to answer due to the faster-growing skills of AI and other technologies and the lack of available labor for performing specific kinds of roles. As we have already learned, there was fear even back in the 1900s about computers taking over our jobs. But with ultra-intelligent AI that we can see is visually able to outperform humans in some of the most complex tasks possible, the question is now becoming more important.

Google's AlphaGo was able to beat the world champion at one of the most challenging games on Earth, called Go, which requires knowledge of millions of different sets of moves to master and extensive training. Just like the game of Go, many jobs are the same, and some that may take humans decades to master can take AI seemingly hours to. So the question remains: Can AI take over all our jobs?

AI and the Society Part 1:
The Smartest Employee
in the World

With gigantic leaps made by AI and the flabbergasting abilities possible with it, the age-old question still is coming back only to huant us with possibly much less appealing results. Labor costs over the years in developing nations have skyrocketed. Just like the inflation of gas, food, houses, and other products, the cost of labor has also followed this response. When the price of goods goes up, people's wages also have to increase in comparison to the goods that people need to purchase to survive. The wages of people have substantially increased in recent years in proportion to inflation. Instead of the wage increase for the worker increasing by around 3.5 percent, it has, as of the writing of this book, increased by 6.49 percent, which is about two times higher.

Labor across all sectors is becoming much more expensive, even in sectors that you may not realize pay that much importance to the economy. Having employees in developed countries and also in more expensive states is becoming so expensive that it is provoking many businesses to jump ship in one way or another. Whether it is relocating from Silicon Valley to Houston or pushing for more remote work employees, startups are becoming more cost-conservative now than they have ever been. Employers now have become ever more reliant on foreign labor in developing countries such as China, India, Bangladesh, Nepal, Turkey, Bulgaria, Armenia, and others. Underdeveloped countries earn much less than developed nations do, and their employees also expect to get fewer benefits from their employers.

In the US, employees in every sector are entitled to fair working conditions, retirement and medical benefits, and sick, maternity, and paid vacation leave. In other countries, employees work for the bare minimum that is legal, with usually very poor or dangerous working conditions, to have a job that would pay them higher in comparison to what most companies in their home country would pay them. You can see this by simply searching up the average living wage for a certain country online. The minimum wage per hour in India is just over $2 USD, whereas in the US, in most states, the minimum wage is about $17 per hour. Over the course of a month, the differences in earnings can be substantial. The foreign employee earning $2 USD an hour will, over the span of a month, earn about $300 if working 40-hour weeks. The American employee, on the other hand, who may earn about $17 an hour, will instead earn about $2,300 a month. The living conditions that can be afforded with these two different paychecks are quite astounding.

This is why many activists have complained about the exploitation of foreign labor, and political debates have made factory and autoworker jobs being pushed out of the country a major national issue. Many people, even those in foreign nations, still oppose the poor pay and the possibly dangerous working conditions that their jobs may require them to perform in. It can take a major toll on a person's health. Yet corporations, on the other hand, require this low-cost labor to function properly. If an automaker, for example, decided to relocate its main production facilities to the US from China, it would have to pay its employees tens of thousands of dollars more for its technicians in the US than it would have to in Asia.

This raises a concern. Is there a way for companies in developed nations to get cheap labor without taking a toll on people's well-being and possibly lives? Well, now with the advent of AI, this goal may be able to be reached. AI can work nonstop around the clock. AI does not need to be paid salaries or given any kinds of medical benefits or vacation. It can perform the most grueling of work without suffering any kind of injuries. Can this mean that AI can take over our least desired jobs? Yes, and no.

As we have seen, AI has the capability to do almost any cognitive task, whether it is thoroughly reading through a text or mastering some of the world's most difficult cognitive sports such as chess and Go. However, its cognitive abilities still have flaws. To begin with, AI will never be entirely human, no matter how much development is done on it to get it there. AI will always be an algorithm running on some kind of a machine that will need to be told what to do through code.

The inability to make assumptions based on intuition, as humans can, given subconscious information piecing itself together to create a solution to an otherwise unfamiliar problem, will not be as strong in AI as it is in people. AI algorithms, as we have already learned, do have an ability of chaos, such as in the GAN algorithms when it comes to generating a pixel arrangement on top of an image made up of the most random assortments of pixels. However, this does not mean that AI algorithms can solely base themselves on chaos.

AI has a much more structured pathway of neural connections in its algorithms than the brains of humans do. AI algorithms need to continue learning in a certain way until it is told that they cannot do so anymore. This same method of learning is the method of any of the algorithms we have learned about, updating weights as the predicted responses to the training data are compared with the real training data. This method does not change over the course of the model learning. While it can be possible for the model to begin learning faster and more accurately as the training goes on, it is part of the process of the model training itself to become more accustomed to the data and therefore causing these results.

In humans, on the other hand, we can suddenly get an insight into a solution that we are facing when we may simply be in the shower or lying in bed looking up at the ceiling. When we anticipate we are doing nothing, our brains are working in the background to solve any problems that we may be facing or come up with new theories about rectified opinions and facts. This happens in our subconscious mind, so when it does occur, we are completely unaware of it and it takes us by surprise.

AI, on the other hand, if it were set in a continuous learning state just like humans, would continue acquiring new concepts and changing old ones based on new information received, but it will not suddenly come up with a completely new insight out of nowhere that it was never given anything close to in the training process for. For example, an AI that was trained on detecting cats from dogs may never be able to guess from suddenly being trained on images of bridges that these images are not cats and dogs if the model is simply given a probability of the image containing a cat or a dog being some number above zero. After all, an image that has even a 0.08 percent chance of being a dog is still a dog compared to an image that is 0.0003 percent a cat. But the AI will never end up understanding that a probability that is this small does not account for the image not containing a cat or a dog. The model, as it is trained on more images of bridges and cats and dogs, will never come to realize this solution, no matter how many images it is trained on.

It is a simple fact that we as humans realize and can learn subconsciously but that AI cannot, no matter how much time has passed. This can leave AI to struggle with certain jobs that may require intuition to perform, such as playing a game of poker. As the AI plays the game, the AI may learn all of the moves that can allow it to win, but it will never be able to fully master the intuition that is involved in the game.

In a regular job, this problem can come about if the AI encounters something that is completely different from anything that it has been trained on or has been trained the wrong way on. The AI may end up making an error on something that its training data simply has not taught it.

The Chinese Room

A very famous test was once performed to test the abilities of an AI to mimic a human in the field of language composition. A subject was placed in an adjacent room to an AI, and both the AI and another human would write a text in Chinese. The subject would then need to guess whether the text was written by the AI or the human. Today's AI can very easily beat this experience with its integrated NLP techniques and generative capabilities. However, does the AI truly understand Chinese? The Chinese language is much more than just writing. Any language, as a matter of fact, is more than just a set of words and letters on paper. These words have meanings, and they have pronunciations.

An AI that is only trained on gigabytes of Chinese texts may never learn how to actually pronounce the words or understand what the words actually mean. Unless the AI is trained on other kinds of data that contain the same words from the data in which the AI was trained for the grammar of the language, the AI will never learn to speak or fully understand the language itself. There may have been many languages throughout history which may have been only spoken or written, but in today's modern society, all of the most widely used languages are used in both forms. If an AI does not have the ability to perform all three tasks, then it cannot become fully fluent in the language. A human, on the other hand, can use their intuition to figure out what certain words mean in a sentence, but they also can learn only one of these skills, such as the ability to write the language and its grammar, before they can begin to understand the spoken form of the language.

This issue is another prohibiting factor to the ability of AI to easily master skills in addition to languages. AI may not always have enough training data to be taught everything it needs to know to perform a task explicitly. It may be given only one part of the total amount of data for a certain task. The model may then be expected to learn to generalize certain actions from there. This confines AI to being held every single step of the way for it to perform a certain task. This can block the ability of AI to perform certain tasks whenever there is not enough data to be able to train them with to perform the task. This will not allow AI to perform certain kinds of tasks with very little information available to train them on, which will either force people to be innovative and create the information themselves from scratch or impede the AI from being fully able to perform the task.

Both these fallacies will not allow AI to perform many cognitive tasks required for jobs. Any kind of jobs that require creativity will require the ability to generalize and have a full understanding of the problem and the skill needed to solve it. When solving a complex problem, this may push AI to either output a solution that has already been written somewhere on the Internet or formulate a weakly based solution to a problem. In a job, specifically one that requires a lot of creativity, this can interfere with the ability of AI to perform many aspects of the job solely by itself.

AI can work well for these roles as an advisor to a human employee but not as a manager or a higher-level role occupant in the profession. An AI will not be able to make decisions primarily by itself without encountering at least one of these fallacies. A human may need to aid the AI frequently with new data to prove it incorrect for it to be able to change its stance on a certain problem. Data is the main inhibiting factor when it comes to AI performing certain roles that we may think it will be able to occupy fully within the next few years. Currently, AI can do the least of what is required for certain creative roles, such as creating a very bare Notes iOS app with purely the basic functionality of a Notes app. It, however, cannot create a notes app that can do more than simply store and retrieve notes for editing.

What if the user may want to send a note to someone else directly from the app? Or maybe change the fonts of the text in their notes? This is what ChatGPT may leave to the developer to do when generating the code for such an app. AI does not know what to expect from a Notes app more than just an app with the basic functionality of a Notes app. AI cannot be more creative than its definition of what a notes app is and the code that can be used to create it. AI cannot change these definitions.

The Problem with Multistep Tasks

Have you ever asked ChatGPT to do something and gotten a response asking you to complete part of the task you have told it to perform? Well, this feature was intentionally made for AI algorithms for them to refrain from doing things that they cannot perform themselves yet. Right now, AI is still very specialized in what it is able to do. LLMs like Bard and ChatGPT may be advertised as the first general artificial intelligence models, but are they really?

General artificial intelligence is a type of artificial intelligence that can perform any task it is given. For example, the AI can perform text summarization tasks, train you to play a chess game, and have a verbal conversation with you. As of this writing, ChatGPT cannot perform any tasks other than verbal, basic cognitive, and text-related tasks. ChatGPT cannot physically get up, walk around the room, or shake your hand. It can perform only a few of the very wide range of tasks out there. A truly generative AI would be able to perform any task that humans can perform, no matter how difficult.

Today, there may be robots connected to advanced AI algorithms that may be able to perform physical tasks, but those robots cannot also perform cognitive tasks at the level of ChatGPT. AlphaGo cannot win a game of chess against Deep Blue, and neither can it win a game of Go against AlphaGo. We are still living in a world of specialized AI. If we want AI to be truly generative, we will need to give it even more data and an advanced base. There is no AI right now that can perform any possible task that a human can perform.

ChatGPT would need a robotic body that it needs to learn to operate for this to happen. Even if we manage to do this, would we even want to? Advancing AI with such big leaps can be dangerous if we do not have the security in place to stop it from being hacked or getting out of hand. We need to first learn how to manage an AI as powerful as ChatGPT right now before we can continue making even greater advances, such as giving it a physical body.

Although even without a body, ChatGPT and other powerful LLMs still cannot perform many tasks by themselves. Apart from physical tasks, AI cannot perform as basic a task as opening a browser or application window and copying and pasting text into it. This is a very easy task for a human to do, but AI still cannot perform it yet. When given a prompt that requires such a task to be done, an LLM would usually suggest you perform any tasks as such or any other tasks that require steps to be taken in a different application or website.

If ChatGPT were a truly generative AI, wouldn't it be able to do this? We discussed in the previous chapter why it might not be a good idea to let AI do this, but without the ability for performing such tasks, AI will not be truly generative. Many jobs require the use of many applications to be used at the same and to be switched in between. On top of this, they may also require certain application windows to also be monitored in case of certain undesired activity in one of these application windows. If AI is not able to do this then, it cannot perform many jobs by itself that we may think it is able to perform.

AI will still need a human counterpart to perform jobs that require opening and monitoring many different applications. Unlike what we might think, ChatGPT is an AI that we still cannot fully see. It sits in one browser window and can only speak or write to us. ChatGPT does not even have full control of a computer yet. This inhibits what ChatGPT can do to a single browser window into only textual and verbal form, and visual form also if you are using ChatGPT for generating images.

What Jobs Are at Risk

With the roadblocks we have discussed, AI will not be able to fully take over many jobs that its proficiency in abilities may match. As with the case of the iOS developer position, the most the AI can do is generate the code for the human developer to then copy and paste into an actual code editor, run the code, check for bugs, fix the bugs, and add any additional functionalities to the code app that the AI may not have anticipated adding. Its ability to code only fulfills one of the skill requirements for being a developer. Its lack of creative ability also inhibits this ability. ChatGPT will not be replacing developers anytime soon, unlike what many may think from its coding and debugging skills.

Jobs that do not require much creativity and are cognitive may be able to be fully performed by AI. Tasks such as copywriting, freelance writing, and freelance digital designing will be the easiest for AI to take over. Writing stands at the highest probability of being fully taken over by AI due to its ability to create texts that are indistinguishable from those of humans in a much shorter time span. Although for longer texts, hiring a freelance writer may still be a better option. AI currently cannot write a two-hundred-fifty-page nonfiction storybook, so you may want to think twice about letting AI write your entire next novel.

Like writing, digital art may also become fully automated with the stunning graphic design abilities of generative AI. AI can create pictures that are indistinguishable from human artwork and can fool even the most skilled art critics. AI can also complete the entire creation of the image directly within your browser window too within only a few minutes. Compared to the cost of hiring a human digital designer, the AI can save thousands of dollars for large-scale projects. Some tasks, like creating a logo or other tasks within the field of digital design that require very high amounts of creativity, may be best left to human designers.

AI can also perform most of the jobs of a lawyer, apart from representation of the person in the courthouse. AI can give very accurate legal advice. The only problem with this is that the stakes for making an incorrect statement are very high. This can result in a much harsher decision being made in certain cases. It is still best, if possible, to hire a real lawyer to be on the safe side. If you are unable to afford the basic service, use cheaper services or free services to still minimize the chance of failure. High-stakes situations are still a downfall for artificial intelligence. The chance of something going wrong outweighing the benefits of a correct decision is the main inhibitor for AI in many different fields. An AI weatherman, for example, stating that a tropical storm heading through the Gulf Coast of Mexico actually turns out to be a third-category hurricane would have much bigger implications than a misspelled word in a document that you have allowed AI to spell-check. AI, as of right now, should be refrained from being used in the highest-stakes situations to avoid technical errors and fallacies from causing overwhelming trouble for the humans using it. This puts off many jobs, such as stock trading and the CEO role, for AI algorithms.

Safer jobs that should be automated by AI are jobs that may be unattractive to humans or are potentially harmful to them. AI is also limited by its physical capability to what jobs it is able to perform. As we have already discussed, there is no AI that exists with the cognitive abilities of ChatGPT and with a body that can operate skillfully. This leaves out jobs such as construction and mining from its reach. AI would create a very meaningful impact if it were to be developed to be able to take over these kinds of jobs. Some of the most unattractive and dangerous jobs for humans are physical jobs. Think about how many dangers are around someone on a construction site. Many materials from the buildings may fall down, and the person may get injured just by walking around there. If AI is taught how to navigate around one of these areas, it can save the lives of many humans. Construction is an unavoidable task that needs to be performed by people. Buildings need to be built, and roads need to be fixed. If AI can perform these kinds of tasks, it can allow the lives of many people working on these kinds of projects to be saved. AI cannot suffer from respiratory failure or hearing loss. It can be put into situations where humans can get injured easily to still get the job done while keeping people safe. AI also will be able to get any physical job done faster than humans due to having only a mechanical body that isn't made up of living cells.

The same skills for doing construction can also allow an AI with a robotic form to perform military work. Wars are one of the most dangerous tasks for humans to engage in, with the highest chance of mortality. The point of a war is to simply destroy the other side until it does not have the capacity to attack, leading to its surrender. The soldiers, though, do not have to be humans. Robots can suffer much more damage than humans before breaking. Robots also can fight tirelessly, and they can acquire extreme physical skills with the right kinds of algorithms. Robots can be trained to outperform humans at any physical task with a strong enough robotic body. However as of today, robots do not currently have the capabilities yet to fight in war, so this will stay only a possibility for now.

What Jobs Can AI Perform in the Future

AI is currently being developed at a breakneck speed, so it isn't possible to tell exactly how far it will be able to go. However, it is possible to make estimates based on the most likely technologies to be developed or enhancements to AI to determine what jobs in the future AI may take over. We already know that some jobs will be more difficult for AI to take over, such as physical jobs. Jobs like construction work, mining, and athleticism may take the longest unless a rapid breakthrough occurs that will allow ChatGPT to control an advanced robotic body. These jobs may even still be around for another one hundred years, depending on the rate at which robotics is developed. So, it is best to say that physical jobs are some of the safest jobs from AI.

Office-related jobs, on the other hand, which are more cognitive, may be able to be taken over entirely by AI, depending on enhancements related to AI to perform a wider range of tasks using technology. Tasks like independently searching the Internet and using software applications on a host device can allow AI to perform all of the necessary tasks required for completing the job without a human counterpart. An example of a simple job that would fall into this category is business intelligence. For more advanced jobs, AI will need a creativity enhancement.

A creativity enhancement would allow a generative AI program to create results that the AI is not trained on. This would mean the generative AI generating a creatively thought-of result without using only the baseline elements of this result. For instance, if the AI receives a query asking for a picture of flowers in the style of Claude Monet, the AI might create an entire garden of flowers, with a lake and sculptures. The garden may not have been explicitly asked for by the user, but the AI can still create it to add more elements to the product.

This is important for the AI to be able to do to create a complete product. Of course, some elements may not be wanted in what AI may create if they are too irrelevant to what the user may want to receive. However, they would provide a baseline for the user to build upon, changing these elements to what they may want to have. It would also allow the AI to learn connections between different elements in the products it creates by receiving feedback from humans on the output it creates. Every time a generative AI model creates a complete result, the user can give feedback to the AI in the form of a number, possibly from one to five, on how well they believe the AI has created the complete result.

Enhancements like this one, and the ability to obtain full access to a computer and the Internet by itself, will give AI the ability to perform a much wider array of jobs in the future. Going back to the job role of an iOS app developer, this would mean the AI being able to make entire apps with all of the functionality a user may request, in addition to some extra features to make the app more complete and accessible. The AI will, from scratch, write code, test the code, debug the code, write new code, launch the app to the iOS App Store, and maintain it after it is launched. These two enhancements would enable AI to complete all parts of a job. The AI will be able to perform the skills necessary to create the product using the entire device and creatively come up with the output.

The Impact on Labor in Developing Countries

At the beginning of this chapter, we discussed the offshoring of jobs like car manufacturing and other factory work to developing nations. Workers in these nations have the advantage of requesting lower pay to do work that Americans and other citizens of developed countries are not willing to do. AI coming in may be the force to change this paradigm. It may not exactly bring back these jobs to developed nations, but it will save the well-being of the people who are currently working in them.

Ever since the Industrial Revolution, factory work has always been despised. The conditions involve working in a crowded, loud building for punishing hours with very few breaks. Sometimes people may also need to operate dangerous machinery, which can even pose risks to their lives. Basic factory work is primarily repetitive, and it may be very easy to automate using AI if AI is given a durable robotic body. Many factories in China have already automated many parts of the process of manufacturing a car. It is primarily the more intellectual work, such as inspecting the car and testing it out, that is still not automated.

This job can be perfect for robots with intelligent algorithms such as ChatGPT to be able to inspect the car's interior and exterior using CNN-like algorithms for processing images on a frame-to-frame basis for detecting any kinds of faults, dirt, or objects that may need to be taken out of the car. With self-driving cars in the future, the car may be able to test itself and provide a detailed report back to humans on what the performance of the car may be through certain obstacles. The humans using this information can determine whether or not the car is ready for being shipped out. This process will insure quicker and higher-quality cars being produced over time, which will eventually make cars cheaper over time. As the production speed remains high, there is a low likelihood that there will ever be low supply unless materials have run out, which may eventually lead to a surplus.

In the long run, robots will save the factory money as they will only need maintenance every few months, and the only cost that the factory will need to pay for maintaining them is simply the cost of their purchase. AI can be the perfect candidate for these jobs as a low-paid employee who can work nonstop and will need no benefits. So what will happen to people in underdeveloped countries who are currently working in these jobs? Similar to how Americans moved on to jobs that require higher levels of skill, employees in developing countries will do the same. Employees will need to focus on jobs that they can perform that will guarantee them good enough pay to live off, which AI has not taken over yet. This may be more challenging than what developed countries have done during the end of the first Industrial Revolution, but there will always be jobs that AI will not be able to perform well enough to take over the entire position.

Currently, the AI automation of factory work has only begun, but as technology continues to advance on top of generative AI, more and more factory work will fall into the hands of robots. While this may seem like a very dark trajectory to the average worker, there are still some positive effects of this revolution. To begin with, developing countries may eventually reach the level of developed countries as their economies grow from the increase in economic output from automated factory work. Faster production means more products and more products mean more buyers. Every time a buyer purchases a product in a certain country, the money goes into the economy of that country. Over time, with the help of globalization, this will allow developing countries to no longer become labor hubs but purely manufacturing hubs. The education will also improve for these countries since more people will need to learn the skills required to enter the technical economy. Eventually, this shift will eliminate almost all global poverty as all countries become equalized under the production capabilities of AI.

The Education in the New Age

With the expansion of skills for certain careers that will not see AI presence for the time being, it is important for students to learn how AI works and how to use it. AI is becoming as important a part of our lives as reading and writing. AI should be taught to everyone everywhere for them to be able to learn the inner workings of one of the world's most important systems. But what exactly could this look like? Can AI have its own class in middle or high school, and if it does, what would it cover?

AI and the Society Part 1: Education for the Future

Imagine you are currently a seventh-grade student. You look at your schedule for the day and see many different subjects, some of which you have picked out of curiosity, others out of passion, and then you have the core classes. The core classes contain all the typical subjects: a math class, a language arts class, a science class, and a history class, but there is a fifth class that is different from the rest. It is much more specialized than all the others and requires you to go to the school's computer lab. You squint closer at your schedule and see that it is a class called Principles of the Ethics of Intelligent Technology.

This class happens to be the first of your school day. You walk to the class and the teacher greets you. She assigns you a seat and you sit in your chair, waiting patiently for the class to begin. At last, the bell comes, and you wait patiently for what the instructions will be. Your new teacher puts a big question on the board: Can AI ever become fully human? You think for a second about the question and begin to realize that while it looks like an easy question, the answer is actually much more complicated than you think. You wait a little bit and then the teacher explains. She states that AI's abilities will never be able to fully compare to humans'. She outlines the reasons for why this is, beginning with the fact that AI is constrained by the data it is trained on, secondly, AI will never be able to perform many mental tasks that humans are able to do, and third, AI will also face other constraints that humans will not have. The teacher finishes by stating that this entire semester will be about answering this question further in detail.

Can this be what the future of education looks like? AI, as we have seen, has very big potential in the economy and in our personal lives. We will very soon interact with AI as often as we read and write. This would beg the question of how people should learn about it. AI is a very big field with many different topics and purposes. AI is not a very simple topic to even be able to map out. In addition to a question about how humane AI can be, there is still a lot more to ask about it. There is so much that even experts don't know about AI. AI also isn't like other subjects. Most other subjects, like mathematics and history, have already been drafted, and most of what you will learn will stay the same over the years. There isn't going to be anything new that gets added to these subjects for very long periods. In the field of AI, this is far from the truth. Day and night, thousands of researchers are constantly adding new insights to the field of AI, whether it be algorithms that may work more effectively for solving a major computational problem or a new theory about how AI can impact a certain industry.

AI is different in many ways from traditional subjects, so this begs the question of how and whether or not it should be taught in secondary schools. This can depend on many factors, like what makes core subjects able to be taught in secondary schools in the first place. For example, in a math class, you learn about the Pythagorean theorem instead of learning about multivariate gradient vectors. Topics taught to students in secondary schools should match the difficulty levels of what students should be learning at their grade level. Students should also be learning only knowledge that is important for their livelihoods in core subjects instead of just any knowledge out there. Core subjects exist in the first place to provide basic knowledge that will allow students to think analytically, understand different basic phenomena, and interact with others through reading and writing. Therefore, they should only provide knowledge about a subject that will actually be used in the real world.

Is It Possible for AI Education to Become a Core Subject

AI is becoming a necessary topic that everyone should learn due to its high importance in our technological society and the possible requirements that may begin to emerge for the future job market. AI education can possibly become a core subject, but there are some barriers to how the subject will be taught that could hinder this from happening. The first is the barrier of grade level to teach AI to beginning nonadvanced students.

For AI to become a core subject, it would need to be made easy for a sixth-grade student to be able to understand, assuming the sixth grader is not already advanced by one or two grades the material needs to be able to be understood by someone without as much knowledge as most of the people who are learning about AI today. Of course, given the enormity of the field, this should not be a challenge, but what about the sixth-grader reading about something, they have no understanding of how it works. The sixth graders most likely would not know anything about AI to begin with so they will be reading about whatever topic in AI given to them from an outsider's perspective. They will have no knowledge of many of the key algorithms and theories involved in it so will they still be able to get a good enough understanding of the material?

Depending on whether or not the student may want to dig deeper into the subject, or they simply may want to imagine how AI may work given what they are learning about in AI, they possibly can, but for those who don't, this may become a challenge. Reading about any topic in which they have zero experience can be challenging for anyone especially if the text covers advanced topics and new research in it. The material will need to be presented using very simple vocabulary terms for many key topics in AI such as for AI itself.

AI as we know it has one overarching definition: a computerized algorithm for learning from data, but to two different people, this definition can mean two different things. If a nontechnical person is reading the definition, they may first wonder what an algorithm may be and what the data may be. They may also wrongly interpret the definition of learning too mistaking it for the type of learning that humans do through verbal exchange or written exchange rather than the method of learning that takes place within our minds. A lack of knowledge about a definition can hinder the ability to be able to interpret the key word. AI in these terms should rather be simply defined as a nonhuman form of intelligence used by computers instead. Since people already understand what intelligence means, and they can easily imagine something that is not human and also something that is used by computers, it would be much more simple for a nontechnical person to be able to grasp the term.

What AI Topics Should Be Taught

As we already know, the world of AI is giant, with many different theories, concepts, algorithms, and methods. It can be quite puzzling to know where to begin. The beginning point of the education about AI will be the most important part of the child's knowledge about the subject because from there they will build up their knowledge to tackle more difficult subjects which may be more important to actually be able to use AI with. A starting topic in most subjects will answer questions such as: What is most important to know? What will have the most use in AI? What will be needed the most to be able to connect the dots and understand AI the best? If a subject can fulfill one of these prophecies, it is a good topic to think about but. However, another factor should also be kept in mind: the subject will be taught to students beginning in sixth grade. Will a sixth grader with their current knowledge of the world be able to understand this topic? If the topic includes knowledge that is too complicated or completely unrelated to anything a sixth grader has ever experienced before or someone has told them about, then it may not be a good starting topic.

When looking over the topics of AI with these questions in mind, the most likely option to be the best topic to start AI education with is a topic on AI and the society. The topic of AI and the society will get students interested and excited about how what their learning connects to the real world and introduce them to the topic. When a student can make a connection between a certain topic that they are learning in school to the real world, they will perform much better on it than just pure theory that we have to accept the way it is without seeing it in action. One of the reasons why students always perform labs or experiments in science is so that they can see the topics that they are learning in action.

Even with the world's most powerful microscope, it is impossible to see an atom. Nevertheless, an atom is the most essential building block of all life and objects on Earth and in the universe. An understanding of an atom is crucial to learning how just about anything within chemistry, physics, and biology operates. Students need to know how an atom works but also be able to actually see it in action. By only learning the theory, a student will be left thinking that they are being forced to believe something that does not actually exist.

Have you ever wondered why so many people today still believe the Earth is flat after hundreds of years of scientific evidence and research stating otherwise? Well, if you ask how many people have actually seen the shape of the Earth, all of them will say that they have only seen it on the Internet. None of them have actually traveled to space and looked at the Earth from afar. If they all did, then they would surely change their minds. A lot of information today is deceiving, and many theories that people have believed for millennia are now being proven wrong. For people to fully believe something that you tell them, you not only need to prove that it is true with logic, such as theory, but you also need to prove it true with experimentation.

In chemistry, for example, months are spent learning about the different types of bonds that types of elements can make with others depending on the amount of protons and electrons each has. Without experimentation, you would not fully believe that this is true, why this would be true, and why you should even be learning this. But when you are given an experiment to do which allows you to actually see how certain substances or elements react together, you begin to see how the theory you have learned makes sense. You get excited; you see how what you have learned actually works in the real world, and then you begin to want to learn more about the topic.

In AI education, the same should be done with topics at any level. At a low level, such as in middle school, this can be easily done by going onto websites or logically thinking about why the theory you are learning is true. At higher levels, such as those taught in high school, this can include actively programming out the algorithms that are being covered, doing projects with test out the algorithms on real data to see them in action, and actually performing the mathematics involved in the algorithms themselves, and performing research on using these algorithms to solve real-world problems from certain datasets. At the highest level (undergraduate, master's, or PhD degree), this would involve performing research on proposing novel types of algorithms or methods for solving problems related to the underlying functioning of these algorithms, writing, and creating mathematical proofs to test out the mathematical theories behind the algorithms, and writing research on them too.

AI is a topic at any level that can be learned through the thorough application of the topic. It is important, when doing this in any topic, to find real-world examples of it or how it can be seen in action in the world around us. For the most basic topic in AI to be seen in action, you can simply observe news feeds from trusted news sites like the *New York Times*, *PC Magazine*, and other national news publications and technology-focused magazines. AI and the world is one of the easiest topics to observe occurring around us right now, even outside of major news sources.

The Most Basic AI Topic Explained

Now that we know where to begin exactly, what will we be beginning with? AI and the world is a very broad category which can mean a lot of different subtopics. Which of those subtopics are good to begin with first and which ones should be ignored all together due to a lack of importance of them to the larger theory of what is being learned?

AI and the world is a definition to describe the many ways that AI can interact with the world in. This can be anything from how children may interact with AI toys, adults interacting with AI in their lives, AI systems built for solving climate change interacting with the environment, or AI changing many important aspects of the economy. All these things may match closely with the definition of AI and the society, but would all of them be necessary to know?

Students in sixth grade may not have the prior knowledge to be able to understand some topics such as how AI is able to swing the stock market unless they have taken a prior economics class or have a general interest in how the stock market works and actively are investing outside of school. This topic may be best to be left for further reading for those who may be interested in how the economy may work. It also isn't crucial, knowing how the stock market, the economy, or any other market is being impacted by AI to be able to understand how does AI interact with the world.

Another topic such as how AI interacts with the environment may be more useful since this is a substantial use of AI in the world that is crucial to be studied for students to be able to learn about one of the most important ways that AI is being used int the world. AI in the environment may also cover some topics such as applications of AI without a thorough examination of them for how AI is able to curb climate change. This can cover anything from smart grids to smart waste management in a simple explanation for how AI can be used to interact with the environment.

Another important topic is AI toys that children can use. This topic will explain how some very popular toys may include AI technologies in them and how students can interact with them in order to be able to stay safe and be able to get the most out of their experience. This topic provides the fundamentals for understanding something that they may interact with daily on a much deeper level, and it also provides them with something that is not very difficult to understand and something that they can very easily experiment with.

Apart from these topics, there are many more that are great candidates for subjects that can be taught in AI education, but these are the ones that can have the most impact on the way that students think about AI going on and how they can see it actually being used in the real world. This is one of the many fact-based topics that can give students a great base to build on in their journey of learning about AI.

In middle school, the topics should be kept out of application to avoid needing to explain complex topics in math. Some more topics that can be taught in relation to this in middle school can include ways that people can stay safe while using AI and ways they can use AI like ChatGPT to the best extent. Factual knowledge will provide the basis for knowledge that will later on include the application of AI algorithms through programming and some basic statistics and algebra.

AI Education in High School

As a high school student, I was shocked to not find one single class in the competitive school that I go to about AI-related topics. Some classes that I have seen and taken before are AP Computer Science Principles, a class that provides the basis for how computers work and AP Computer Science, a class that goes in-depth into basic computer science concepts applied using a popular programing language, Java. It mainly covered topics that are also at the most basic level for being able to understand how to program and also how the inner components of the computer interact with each other. Although there is no specialization of knowledge.

High school is the part of someone's education where knowledge becomes more and more specialized into the interest of the student. For example, a student who really likes science class can take two or even three science classes they would like in addition to the core science class. In the US, high schools have classes which are called electives. They are basically choice classes for what kinds of classes other than the core classes a student would like to take to learn knowledge that they could possibly earn college credit for, and put on their application for college. Of all the electives that I have seen in my school, not one of them covered any topic on AI. This is shocking to see as I would expect there to be some kind of curriculum in place for teaching one of the most important skills of our century.

Not including any extracurricular for AI is like not including any extracurricular for a student who may be interested in history or including any extra curricular for a life skill. Yes, it is true that there definitely would be less students who would be interested in AI than who would be interested in history, but that does not mean that there shouldn't be any option available to them with the recent advent of generative AI, though AI has been thrust into the mainstream.

Before, AI was something that mainly technical people and futurists have discussed in their own circles or something that someone would bring up every now and then, but it has not become something that everyone everywhere is talking about nonstop all at the same time. People now are realizing the capabilities and importance of AI in our society, so it has never been a better time for there to be at least one high school class, whether it is an elective or a core class, to cover artificial intelligence and its applications. Many people, technical or nontechnical, would be thrilled to learn about something that is currently taking the world by storm.

The elective and core classes, of course, will be very different from each other. The elective class will be the first type of AI class introduced into high schools. As of right now, the AI hype has only begun, and while many more people are getting interested in AI much faster, there still aren't enough people and enough industry need for there to be a core AI class that will start from sixth grade and extend to twelfth grade. Not everyone may also want to learn how to code. A key part of seeing how AI works in the real world is actually being able to build it yourself. Being able to build AI yourself is as important to getting a good understanding of AI as experimentation is in physics. It is the key way that you see how everything works and get excited about the subject.

Though, unlike experimentation in science, this kind of experimentation will be much more complex. Programming itself can have its own class. In fact, there are thousands of programming languages in existence today, with eight key languages. Each language has its own unique syntax and function, just like a regular language. Learning one of these languages is not for everyone, and it can also be timely for those who don't have any help when learning the programming language, such as help from technical parents, a technical group, or special resources on or off the Internet. This is why this book primarily focuses on the theory of AI instead of the code to actually create the algorithms. Programming is the next step up in AI for anyone who wants to learn more about it and actually see it in action, but it is not a requirement for understanding how AI works. The theory is enough for you to see today how AI is applied in the real world and how it actually works. Similarly, core classes should not require students to learn programming to understand AI.

The elective class, on the other hand, will focus on learning a programming language, such as the most popular one in the world right now called Python for being able to create the algorithms and see them in action. For an even better understanding, students can use these algorithms in projects such as predicting different diseases from images using algorithms like CNN or LSTM or even generating their own using a GAN. This will make them even more excited about AI, and those with an undecided career path may even end up choosing to major in computer science in college.

The core class, in addition to teaching the algorithms, will also provide real-world examples through no-code methods of building artificial intelligence models. There are currently online tools for anyone who doesn't have knowledge of any programming to use to learn about how AI algorithms work in an application and how to run them. Even in the real world, some companies allow employees to use these tools for various reasons, such as faster time to production or simply to test out an algorithm they want to make without spending excessive time coding it. Core AI classes can also use this tool to cover the same concepts as in a regular elective class but without excessive mathematics or complexity around very specific topics.

A Future of AI Classes

AI, with its many different pathways, will always have choices based on difficulty and interest. Those who are more interested in the subject and who want to learn more about it can take elective classes where the difficulty will remain high along with the amount of materials covered. Bare minimum classes, while they will come to exist later on, will always exist in synchrony with the AI elective classes. AI, as we have seen, has many different types of core algorithms but also many other types of algorithms that may span outward from them. There have been algorithms made for different purposes as versions of different types for solving different problems. AI can be used for many more things than most people can imagine, and the topics that are covered in a specific class should cover the expectations and the interests of the student. Many different elective classes can be created that can focus on specific topics of AI, such as NLP for students who may want to learn about the basis behind ChatGPT, or image generation, where a student can learn about GANs to learn how to enhance artwork they make or learn how to create detailed artwork using AI.

Core classes will never override AI elective or interest classes, so students will not get bogged down by only being limited to what they are being taught in the core classes. Core classes without any elective classes will make the subjects look much duller than they actually are. The creators of the IB program, a program that is offered in high schools, know this well. Higher-level classes that very few people take but still exist, such as IB Further Maths or IB Chemistry L2, are classes whose existence is questioned for their rigorous difficulty and distance from the material being taught in the core classes. However, they are a great example of elective classes that someone can even take as credit for core classes. Interest classes for a student who may want to learn more about the subject being offered in the core IB classes or those that are at the most basic level to learn more challenging concepts, giving them a deeper understanding of the field. This is especially beneficial for someone who may be studying the subject for their bachelor's degree.

The Most Important Topic for AI Education

What is the last thing you remember from high school? Is it the method of differentiation or the process of nuclear fusion? Many peo-ple will remember barely anything, if anything at all. People change a lot over time, and life demands more and more of our attention as we grow older. Many people, even students, forget what they have learned over a single summer. This is the reason that most advanced classes in specialized topics have a period of review time to go over basic material that may have been forgotten in one or two years. Knowledge that is going to be remembered needs to be repeated over and over again and needs to be presented in a way that students can easily remember.

Every core class has many things that you may need to remember to be able to use the skills taught in the class later on in life. Similarly, AI education needs to have something that students will remember in the future from their classes, something that will help them navigate life around artificial intelligence. Students need to have a reason for learning the basics in the first place apart from just understanding AI. So what can this be? Think about how people interact with AI on a general basis. Unless they become software developers, people will not need to know the very basis of the algorithms for their entire lives or the theory behind them. The core of being able to interact with AI properly should be what students remember most coming out of this class.

The core of AI would be many key topics together, such as knowing exactly what to say or write to an AI or how to complete certain tasks using it. But the most important thing about AI interaction that we are even in need of today is education on misinformation. AI has taken the world by storm and is only to continuing to advance, with very few people understanding how it works, making misinformation very easy to get away with. Think about how hard it may be to spot a fake video of a presidential candidate during an election.

During the 2016 presidential election, there was an exodus of fake videos of the nominees for both parties. This led people to become confused and eventually give up on voting altogether, not choosing to support or trust either side. Deep fakes and other forms of misinformation using AI can be much more damaging and difficult to spot than anyone could imagine. Now more than ever, it is time that people learn about their effects, how to spot them, and how to stop them.

AI and the Society Part 2: A Misunderstanding About Misinformation

Misinformation has existed ever since politics have existed. Misinformation began when the first political elections were held to mislead the supporters of the opposing party into believing information that is slightly or very altered from the truth, which may swing their support from their current party. This information existed in the form of propaganda, using information to the benefit of emotion and sensation to achieve political goals, whether during an election or to keep support for a current party in power. This type of misinformation then became the medium for other forms of lying and deceit over time.

The notion of fake news, though, in the advent of technology, has gone wild. In the past, fake news, such as news relating to the Spanish flu pandemic's medication being infected by Bayer, a German company, during the midst of the First World War when the US was fighting against Germany, spread in social gatherings or newspapers. Misinformation spreads very slowly, and some people might go without ever even hearing about the misinformation at all. Today, it is a completely different story. In a tipping economy and in a state where democracy is no longer the same as it used to be, misinformation never has had a better time and reason to go wild.

This can be seen with the numerous instances of presidential elections or any political election in developed countries across the world being tampered with deep fakes and misinformation coming from certain news outlets on both sides of the political spectrum.

In the corporate world, it can be seen with companies like Nikola Motors and Theranos being charged with fraud over technology that investors put their money into, believing it to be real and revolutionary, only to find out that it was all fake and the technology had never even existed or worked, to begin with. In the social world, this can be seen with people applying filters to themselves on sites like TikTok and Instagram to hide what they truly look like and adding pricey props that they themselves don't originally own.

One very famous example of this is the private plane prop in Los Angeles, where tourists can pay a small fee to enter and spend some time in it. This "private plane" is not even a plane; it is the body of a plane that cannot be flown with a very fancy interior. This prop was originally built for movies where a scene with the interior of a private plane would be necessary for the plot of a movie. Over time, because of its realism, influencers began flocking to this model plane for taking selfies to attract attention of their followers and other people on social media for believing that they actually have flown on a real private jet. In a world where it is possible to get almost anything that you want, it has never been easier to fool other people into believing what you think or what you are doing.

People will always flock to something that sends off a signal of extreme emotion. In the example of the private plane model, people seeing an image of someone in a private plane may become interested in the person in the picture, thinking that they may be very wealthy or have special connections. In addition, this is not even the only way to fake this experience. For those who don't live in Los Angeles or don't want to travel there, apps are available on the app store that can be used for booking private planes for short flights for under $1,000 a person. Wherever there is an opportunity, entrepreneurs will step in to make the opportunity cheaper, allowing for any experience to be affordable for people in developed countries. This in itself has only helped the crisis of misinformation to grow. In a world where people are vying for attention, wealth, and power, misinformation could never have a more perfect base to grow on top of.

Envy also is a key driving force, especially among younger and ambitious people. When someone sees the high achievement or experience of another person, they may feel an excessive need to one-up them for their own personal comfort or to prove the person wrong. People who may be envious of the influencer who had taken a photo of themselves in the private plane may even try to one-up them by trying to make a more realistic image of themselves in a private plane or get onto a fancier private plane to take a photo on. This is what has led to misinformation over time becoming more and more realistic. On top of this, people have also used this as an opportunity to make a business selling products that can help people lie about experiences on social media with very high success rates to get their desired outcome.

Only recently, though, there has been a big new entrance of a free product into this space that none of the most expensive products can compete with. This new product is as easy to use as writing a message to someone asking them to do something. The product is obvious given its definition. AI is notorious for creating images and videos that can be as far from the truth as possible and look as realistic as possible. No tool, no matter how expensive, before the advent of ChatGPT and large language models could be able to compete with it. ChatGPT is the king of all photo and video editors in its ability and intelligence. I already mentioned how digital artists are being taken advantage of with AI. It is very difficult to tell whether a piece of digital artwork was created by an AI algorithm or not. This can go for even images containing real people. OpenAI had to add constraints to the content ChatGPT can make, so because of this, people will not be able to make false media content of famous people performing acts that may be inappropriate or illegal. OpenAI already prevented thousands of queries from executing, suggesting ChatGPT make an image of a famous person performing a certain action. While it isn't said yet whether this is the same with written media content, there will still always be AI models that will allow people to misuse them, especially if these models require a subscription. Deep fakes, unfortunately, pay not only to the reputation of the person shamed in them but also to the company that created the AI chatbot that made the deep fake, either by subscription or by paying per use of their image generation algorithms. AI deep fakes have simply been made to work for profit.

A Perfect Environment for Information Overload

With the Internet, it is possible to connect with someone from the exact opposite part of the world in seconds and send messages to them in seconds. Social media platforms such as Facebook, Instagram, and X (formerly Twitter) have all contributed to this. But social media wasn't always so bad. Of course, there are good sides to social media, such as the way it can give you the ability to connect with a relative you haven't seen in person for ten years in less than a second, but in the past, nearly 97 percent of the problems of today's social media were nonexistent. One of these problems is inappropriate content. It may be difficult today to imagine a time when social media was clean enough for a five-year-old to scroll on without seeing any harmful content.

In the past, social media was centered around only certain topics. For example, Facebook, when it first existed as a site for college students, allowed them to socialize and share media. Yes, there was inevitably some harmful content on it, as with any platform created for socializing, including in-person platforms, but in the past, there was much less. Facebook, in its early days, was used by college students at Harvard who wanted to meet with each other more quickly than walking across campus to see each other face to face. Students on Facebook were easily able to go onto their 1980s-style PCs and chat with each other over the site. At first, students began to talk about school-related subjects and formed study clubs on the site. Students would usually exchange content that was centered around group projects and study content for exams.

Over time, as word of mouth began to spread about Facebook started to spread, more students began to use the site, allowing for a more diverse kind of activity to enter onto the site. Students began to use the site as a dating platform, as it was a much easier way to exchange messages without any kind of in-person interaction. Students started forming groups designated to different activities on the site to create specialized groups where they can communicate with other people on social media for the reasons that they were on it. Within these groups, users began to feel free to post whatever they have wanted with a feeling that they may be able to better hide any messages that they may write to one another within a group or through private messaging from the main feed.

As Facebook's user base began to rapidly expand, more and more people turned to this method of communication for sensitive information and began taking advantage of it. Users began to share not only content that they would like to be kept private to each other in this method. People began using it also for sharing inappropriate and harmful content. As millions of people suddenly have joined the platform, some of the activities that they have started to do on the platform became questionable. People viewed social media as a quick unregulated method to exchange any kind of information over the Internet that they have wanted. All kinds of groups, from government organizations to terrorist groups, began to join the platform from all over the world.

When Facebook reached about two billion users, the problem of unregulated content began to reach its tipping point. Facebook began to receive many messages about adult content and verbal assault on the sites along with content depicting violence. With so many users, Facebook found itself in mud having to deal with creating a method to moderate content from over a hundred countries all over the world in hundreds of different languages. The inactiveness though changed after the over throw of a political ruler in Southeast Asia. Many political groups use Facebook as their main site for organizing events. The power of online media had never been greater, with more people having access to it than ever before in history.

The platform had become so big that knowing even where to begin has become a challenge and Facebook's recommendation algorithms have only made it worse. With so many different types of content and hundreds of millions of people using the site at once, it is nearly impossible to be able to apply moderation to all of the content at a fast-enough speed so that nobody sees any harmful content after it gets posted. There is no method of fact-checking and checking for content violation rules or anything else. This is why multicontent sharing platforms like Facebook have become the breeding ground for extremist movements and inappropriate content. If there was a way that Facebook would be able to be moderated it would be used but there aren't any methods that can be very effective in the case of checking the content in a speedy way after the user posts it onto the site and make little error with distinguishing harmful content from content that is okay to post.

Dealing with Misinformation

With so many key factors in the creation of misinformation being present, it is impossible to escape encountering it when you are anywhere online. The best thing you can do is know what to do when you encounter it. Misinformation can range from videos to speeches; there are hundreds of different types of information that can be faked online, but each of these different types of fake information share characteristics that make it quite distinguishable from real information. Fake information, as we already know, is most likely created with the help of AI to obtain as much accuracy and speed in production as possible. AI is currently one of the main driving forces behind misinformation, so looking for similar flaws in different deepfake works, similar to the problems that could be experienced with any AI-created content, can give you a hint about its realism.

AI-created pictures may be missing certain details such as straight fingers or small details in the background. The process of GANs generating images over a latent noise space will not allow for all of the items in the image to be completely precise due to possible fallacies in the AI algorithm or in the training set of the images. AI-generated images can also have a watermark if the training set can contain images that were created by artists who have applied watermarks to their work. Some other ways that misinformation can be detected are through filter application on an image if you tend to download it. Images are generally the easiest type of misinformation to detect due to their intricacy in displaying information. An image can tell much more than a piece of text or a speech. The latter two are much more difficult to detect fallacies in.

Text may be the second most widespread form of misinformation on the Internet. Since text is primarily used to convey news and is usually what information people would turn to when wanting to learn about an important political event. Text created by AI is even more difficult to distinguish in its accuracy. The text contains words, and it is up to the reader to interpret the idea behind the information given, so fallacies may not be as obvious. In the text, since the image is portrayed by how the reader interprets the text, it is best to decide whether or not the text includes an extremist position on a specific subject and to analyze the source of it. A fake piece of text describing a certain natural disaster may include much more extreme language to portray the outcome of the natural disaster.

For example, a hurricane that may have hit Tampa Beach, which has never happened, could be described in a fake piece of text as being a catastrophe of *unseemable proportions* that could have easily been prevented by more government intervention. This piece of text is easily seen as biased. Hurricanes are not a once-in-a-lifetime event; in fact, Florida usually receives four to five hurricanes every year during its hurricane season, likely one of which is a category 5. The piece of text refers to a disaster that seems far more severe by stating the words *unseamable proportions*. The text also connects the hurricane event to a response from the government, giving you a sign about the purpose of the text. In any piece of propaganda, whether written by an AI algorithm or a person, the purpose of the text will almost always be very clear. The point of any propaganda is to change the viewer's mind about a specific topic or to strengthen their belief in it, whether for good or bad reasons. In the case of misinformation, the purpose will usually be negative since the opinion will most likely be based on lies.

In the text, the purpose is clearly to make the reader believe that the government is responsible for a poor response to a natural disaster that it has described as being terrible and extraordinary. In a fact-based piece of text, there will be less emotion, and the point of the text will be less obvious. A news article, for example, explaining the damages of a real hurricane that hit Miami, may instead go into detail about the survivors of the hurricane and what they have experienced. The reader would be left to determine from reading the experiences of the survivors to determine what is the key point of the article instead of it explicitly telling it. The language would also not be very emotional since the logical facts will convey the reason for believing in the text. Neither humans nor AI can get around this common fallacy, so if you think that a piece of text is AI-generated, look for these indicators.

Speeches are the most difficult to determine as either true or false. Speeches are audio versions of text; they may include similar indications of being propaganda or being created by AI as text, but speeches have another characteristic that can help people instill belief in them: voice intonation. Voice intonation is a very important part of speech for conveying its message. Someone may be more likely to believe a speech about a political viewpoint if extreme anger or sadness is used in the voice tone. However, AI is not as good at doing this in audio as it is in text. AI can struggle with perfectly matching the voice intonation of a speech due to the wide range of vocal cords that a person may exhibit along with matching their voice perfectly.

In the same way that AI can unknowingly add some unwanted features in generated images, which may give away the fact that they are AI-generated, it also does this for audio. Someone's voice being very monotonous may be a good example. In a speech, people usually use emotion to convey certain kinds of events. If in a speech someone is not displaying a lot or any emotion, this can be a giveaway about where the video has come from. A person's voice is also very specific and hard to replicate by AI. In any person's voice, whether it may be that of a singer or a politician, their voice will have numerous different intonations that will make up the audio ranges for the speech. Some AI models, such as CNNs, because of their max pooling mechanism, skip over some details in the audio files during the processing and lose details that would make it up.

The max pooling mechanism is meant to take the max value in a field of the training data, whether it is an audio file or an image, and place it into a more extrapolated form of the data to allow it to eventually fit into a neural network. While the change may seem very small in the case of losing only a few milliseconds of audio, the effect is very noticeable when you listen. It is very easy to tell the difference between high-quality music and low-quality music. Likewise, the same is true for any kind of audio.

Videos, which are the most explanatory way of explaining information, are the easiest to determine the purity of. Videos have many more methods of an AI model messing up than even images do. Videos are a time frame of many different pictures spanning different lengths in time. When a phone takes a video, it actually takes pictures at a rate that is so fast it is not noticeable to the human eye. This is why, when a video is running slowly, it can seem like it has stopped working. In this case, it isn't the video that has stopped working; it is the picture transitioning mechanism.

For AI to generate a video, it needs to create thousands or millions of different images that would contain different segments of the video and connect them all together into an MP4 or related container file. This would also be done for the sound of the video, too, if it has any. The connections between the images that make up the video are where the curtain starts to unfold. AI-generated images already can have many problems, such as too many or too few fingers on a person or a vase in the background that looks like a cloud. Making connections between these faulty images will only make the faults look more apparent, along with introducing more faults to the scene.

If a person in an AI-generated video were to move across a room while swinging their arms right next to them, the AI algorithm would struggle with creating the connections between the scenes of the faulty representations of the fingers on the person. The fingers would most probably glitch and give an unappealing characteristic to the video, which would immediately be noticed. The vase in the background may also begin to glitch or stretch without reason, giving another strange element to the video. Videos with these characteristics are almost certainly generated by an AI algorithm.

The addition of audio in the video can only help the process of AI-based video generation to become even more faulty. Most videos, especially those containing propaganda, are likely to contain audio to help the message become even more important. This would indicate another thing to look for in AI-generated deepfake videos. The problems with the segments of audio potentially being connected together, if the video is long, along with the same problems surrounding the creation of audio alone, create the perfect method for a noticeably fake piece of AI-generated content.

Video generation is currently one of the newest fields of AI, which is still being intensively developed. Generative AI has recently played a big role in enhancing the quality and the avoidance of error, but it has not eliminated it entirely. It is true that AI will continue to generate stronger and stronger results over time, but just like anything that is made purely from technology, it will inevitably have problems.

Potential Solutions

Misinformation may be a very big issue that will be very difficult to solve but not impossible. Misinformation is a problem that is mainly centered around users using AI algorithms (and some using their own imagination and skills) to create falsified content for spreading lies and propaganda. Most of the information has the same source of creation, so it can be possible for one single algorithm using artificial intelligence to be able to detect this kind of content. Content that is generated in this way may be very difficult for humans to be able to decipher alone for determining the validity, but for AI algorithms it is a breeze. It is possible for algorithms to be able to take apart AI-generated content to look for certain aspects that may preclude to a chance that the information is fake for us. Key aspects of propaganda or giveaways that may be more difficult for humans to spot which AI can detect with ease.

For example, a feature of slight distortions in an image that has one main focus may lure the attention of the viewer toward the part of the image containing the main details, such as a figure in the middle of it. A slight distortion in the image background, especially if it is entirely the same color, may be difficult for a human to detect. However, AI with convolutional neural networks can detect such an abnormality, no matter how small or big. An AI model which is trained on many images or other kinds of data with the typical faults of AI-generated content of that type can detect these same abnormalities in any type of data which is fed into it. Wherever there is a pattern in data, AI algorithms can excel and pull insights from it to compare the insights about it to data that it has been trained on to make an inference. Misinformation follows this exact pattern.

It may even be possible to detect misinformation before it goes out onto the Internet. Automated machine learning systems can be made to scan each post that can be posted onto a social network after a user hits the post button. The algorithm will scan different kinds of information in the user's post, such as the image, text, and audio, to make sure the content of it do not contain any information that may be false. The algorithm can even find the correct information from online and it can provide the user with it if misinformation is detected in the post in case the user doesn't know the information they are posting is false.

Misinformation can be so misleading that many people who originally may think that the information was false and irrational may start believing it is true if they see enough of it. Most people, in fact, begin believing in fake news this way. If the AI system can give them the correct information and a reason why it is correct, the user can potentially change their mind. AI can go even further with a solution. AI can evaluate the trustworthiness of different sites and provide the user with a detailed explanation of why content in a user's post is incorrect, along with the trustworthiness of the sites where the information to prove this is pulled from. To change their mind or know that what they believe is untrue, people need a logical explanation along with the right sources that back it up. AI can provide a detailed enough analysis to teach anyone who has even been only introduced to misinformation online why it is correct in a detailed enough way so there can be enough evidence for the truth to be proved.

If AI is deployed across all platforms and given the task of detecting misinformation, it may be able to solve the problem. In the future, as developments are continuing to come along, AI will eventually reach this threshold. But even if we solve the problem of misinformation, another problem seems to arise. How much improvement to AI is too much? So far, we have primarily talked about cases of humans using AI to solve problems; we haven't talked about AI solving problems all by itself and what may happen if we let it do that.

With AI's high cognitive capabilities, its ability is indeed very high. It can possibly solve many of the world's problems if we allow it to, but should we? The more abilities we allow AI to have, the more we are letting its influence grow as it outperforms humans across many fields, and the higher the risk for a small mistake or a hack to cause a catastrophe. How many abilities are too much for AI? How much influence of AI is too much? Is it possible for AI to safely take up major positions of power to aid humans to solve the world's problems?

AI and the Society Part 2: AI Governance?

Imagine going out to vote in the presidential election. You currently have three candidates to choose from: one is a candidate from the Democratic Party, the second from the Republican Party but the third one seems kind of strange. This candidate has only a first name, Katy, but no last name. Surprised, you wait until the evening to watch the debate. You suddenly see who the candidate Katy is when she comes out onto the stage. It turns out she is an intelligent robot created to serve as a politician. The robot has served so far on the board of the EPSA with a successful tenure and has implemented all kinds of innovative and well-thought-out solutions to solve some of the biggest environmental decisions in a world where climate change is currently taking the stronghold. Katy has been created as a collaboration between researchers at many innovative government agencies and large tech companies. Katy has an intelligent generative AI cognitive core and has been trained on data from history dating back thousands of years on rulers from thousands of different kingdoms and dynasties. Katy also has been trained on data from the speeches of all the presidents of the US in history and their debates to learn how to properly construct a speech using NLP and generative methods. Listening to her positions on many major issues discussed in the presidential debate, you admire Katy's solutions to many political issues and her straightforward responses to proposals from the opposing party. You begin to think that she could become a great president for the US, but you stop and wonder to yourself if AI can really govern a nation properly.

A hypothetical scenario like this one may not be as dystopian as we might imagine. It is becoming more and more difficult to find quality candidates for political offices and even more difficult to convince some of the world's most intelligent, wise, and successful people to run for a political position. With a lack of quality candidates, citizens are beginning to suffer from poor decisions made by them. The political atmosphere today is not the same as it was just ten years ago. The world was much more peaceful, it was more simple (in some ways), and the differences between people were not as large as they have become recently. It seems like one of the most important jobs is suddenly becoming one of the most vacant due to the stigma around it and the stress of the job.

The problems that citizens face from this are a lack of policies being made to counter important issues, a lack of improvements made to fix things that are not working, and a lack of say in how and what these policies will be. It is visible to see many of these problems across developed nations today. With these issues remaining in place, the quality of life in the nation suffers and potential rivals to the nation may become stronger. So what can be done about it? Well, maybe we should look to Katy. AI has the power to perform many of the actions that a politician has, such as the ability to form speeches, figure out solutions to difficult problems, and learn about what is going on that they may need to attend to. AI can be a potential answer to finding a perfect candidate for a political office, but is it?

Letting AI gain too much influence can backfire if it happens to make even a small mistake. AI is not human, and it can never be fully human. Allowing AI to be able to go off to do something alone may not be a good choice. ChatGPT is a good example of a powerful AI that people have done all kinds of experiments with out of curiosity, media attention, or fun. People asked ChatGPT all kinds of silly questions or questions about unrealistic things. The AI has always responded to these questions in a rational way, completely ignoring any kind of differing incentive the user may have originally intended the AI to answer with. ChatGPT has also answered some questions inappropriately if it was not originally trained on data related to a query a user has typed in, or it hallucinated a response to the user's query that made no sense based on data the model has already been trained on.

If asked a basic question that a human may not know an answer to, a human will probably reply that they don't know or they are not sure. AI, on the other hand, may output an incorrect answer to the question because it may have been trained on data that it believes includes the answer to the user's question. This makes AI prone to making mistakes, which can have radical consequences if it holds a position of power. Mistakes in some negotiations, especially with rivals, can result in war or the breaking of important treaties. In other cases, it can cause a person who may otherwise be innocent to be found guilty or vice versa. Every single decision in a position of power matters, so AI in its current state is not ready for that big of a responsibility.

People in positions of power must have humanity in them to make decisions that would harm the least amount of people. People in power have the responsibility over the lives of the people they affect with the decisions they make and the people who are carrying out the plan for the decision. Protecting any of these people should be the number one priority for a person in power to realize. AI in this context may have a difficult time. Optimization problems or problems where the main goal is to be able to think about the correctness of the outcome based on the allocation of resources. The product being optimized is based on the importance of it to the outcome of the problem. An example of an optimization problem can be: maximizing the area of a garden. These kinds of problems are generally not very difficult for people to solve, as the importance of different items in a certain problem is usually straightforward. However, when the importance of different objects is not certain, the problem can become more challenging. For example, when two groups of objects share the same level of importance but cannot be prioritized at the same time.

Imagine a self-driving car needing to choose between crashing into a couple walking across the street or crashing into a street pole due to the lack of space on the road. Situations like this may be rare, but in politics, they are very prevalent. There are many times compromises may need to be made between two parties, and most of these compromises involve high stakes. The entire purpose of politics is to find a method for pleasing all parties. AI relies on the developer to teach it what are the important features of a certain problem out of the training data. The developer can train an AI algorithm on different optimization problems, initially giving it the answers for different problems and allowing it to learn the patterns for them, but each problem is unique. The lack of common sense in AI that humans possess doesn't allow it to make accurate decisions in optimization problems that it hasn't been initially trained on. Humans may be able to estimate the importance of two parties that may originally look the same based on their experiences and their own common sense, but AI is confined to relying on the training data to decide this. The issue of the lack of common sense is also matched with a lack of human dignity, which may hinder its ability to make proper and safe decisions.

One of the main problems that faces AI is the inability to be able to make decisions explicitly which would favor the well-being and lives of humans which is especially important in the field of politics. This issue is caused by the same reason for the fault of AI to be able to make decisions based on common sense. AI unless explicitly told to may make decisions based on what it believes is more logical instead of what would be best for people or to solve the problem. In a field such as politics, a lot can go wrong if the only way of measuring a choice is by the logic of it. It may seem logical, for example, to use nuclear weapons in a conflict to end it much sooner instead of continuing to send troops to the enemy country to die in battles, but the latter option would prevent the loss of the lives of the citizens of the country and also decrease the risk of retaliation by the opposing nation.

Logic is only one part of the solution to any complex problem. Logic is one of the frames for the solution to a problem by picturing the rationality for this solution. But a good solution to a problem also requires humanity, considering whether or not a problem will benefit the people and the parties involved, the consequences of the outcome of what the solution to the problem will cause after it is implemented, and also the need that this problem satisfies the requirements or restrictions that are in place for solving the problem. If the answer is yes, then the solution is optimal. AI doesn't use this exact kind of reasoning for solving a problem. Apart from not using humanity as one of the frames for a good solution, it also does not consider the aspects of consequences and restrictions. It requires the consequences to be told to it beforehand, or for a similar problem, it has been trained to contain the consequences of the action. It also cannot infer any restrictions for the solution just from being told a problem alone. The restrictions also need to be provided to it by the user. AI is constrained in making decisions for major problems because of this. AI, in this context, will need to be utilized alongside humans to do the job safely and correctly.

The Barriers to AI Governance

With improvements in AI, politicians may seem like something that is doable, but for it to become a reality, people need to be willing to allow AI to serve in government positions on par with humans, which is very unlikely to happen. There is a very big stigma around AI and AI governance due to conspiracy theories and other fears about what it might produce. One of the main fears to doing this is the rise of nuclear weapons being produced that can cause total annihilation of both sides in any war where they are utilized.

During the Cold War, we have seen something like this similar happen when the US and the Soviet Union were caught in a rapid arms race to try to build more deadly, stealthy, and quick weapons that they could hurl at each other and their allies whenever provoked far enough. As the weapons were being produced, each country tried to slightly push the other back and move their weapons closer, just in case they needed to fire them. This caused the Cuban Missile Crisis, which was the intense fear of Soviet missiles being fired into the continental US after the Soviet Union moved them into Cuba and US missiles were placed in Turkey. The risks remain high of this kind of scenario happening again today, only with much more powerful weapons. People are not very comfortable knowing that one glitch in the device hosting the AI algorithm can cause it to make a decision that can make a nuclear war happen. As we have already mentioned, humans need to be in supervision of AI at all times, and the humans need to be in charge of carrying out the decisions that the AI would propose after evaluating that they would be safe, rational, and restraint filling, and carry consequences that can be handled although people would still not be satisfied enough to allow for AI governance to occur.

In addition to the fear of nuclear war, people may also fear that AI will show a big disregard for citizens and implement draconian laws that may undermine people's sense of freedom and humility out of the rationality of such laws being enacted. People are worried that things that are innate by human nature, an AI may declare to be dangerous and irrational and can try to suppress the doing of these activities. There are many current actions that people may do that may seem irrational to an AI algorithm who may deem the action to not be logical. Something small that may not be normal, an AI algorithm in a position of power may want to deem illegal due to it being improper in the logical sense or to risks it may overestimate. People who are overly scared of AI may also make up false claims about the purpose of AI wanting to be put into power to do this. Conspiracy theories are taking major hits around the humility and trust in AI and the ideals for it being put into power. People may also think that the people who have created AI may intentionally want to put it into power to harm citizens. People don't realize that AI can only do things that it is instructed to do and that humans can work alongside the AI to ensure that whatever decisions it makes fit the criteria of a humane, risk-averse decision. People believe that AI is a rogue force, like a Terminator-like robot, that is waiting around the corner to stage an attack on someone unknowingly. AI is instead an intelligent algorithm that is constrained by what it is trained on and by the user query regarding what it can do. Even if one day AI within the body of a robot can stand on two legs, it will not be able to just wander around the room and do whatever it wants. It will need some kind of purpose, which its algorithm will be designed around. This algorithm will dictate what kind of data it will use for its base knowledge and what it will be able to know and learn. The risk of rogue AI that could become harmful can easily be mitigated by simply training it on data that doesn't include any knowledge of anything that may increase the chance that it does harm. The system and the data alone, though, are not enough by the developer to be crafted to not allow any harmful actions to take place.

People are also worried about the chances that an enemy nation may attack an AI in power to change its algorithm and training data to include harmful decisions or actions that can cause a dangerous outcome for the nation. The hacking of systems from other enemy nations has grown more and more common in recent years, especially since technology in all nations is becoming more powerful.

There has recently been an upheaval of cyberattacks that have been occurring for military efforts by opposing nations especially in times of war. Russia's cyberattacks on Ukraine are an example or the interference into voting systems in one country is also such. On top of this, more and more of a nation's most precious data is being stored on one of the least safe platforms: the Internet. This has begun to invite a new type of warfare. Instead of directly attacking a country by sending troops along with heavy artillery and weapons, why not simply attack them online? Almost every single technology to date is connected to the Internet or is part of a process that is used to access the Internet. Many new technologies make it even easier for unprotected devices to be broken into. Placing too much precious data on any technology alone is dangerous, and AI is no exception. The database of commands that an AI could store in its short-term memory, which may contain ongoing conversations that it could be taking part in, may be able to be broken into. When any large language model-based AI algorithm is operating, it requires some kind of data to be stored in short-term memory, such as in an LSTM how this would be done, by updating the weights. There need to be better measures for securing the databases holding ongoing conversations running on the AI if using them, or better methods to safeguard the operating systems that the robot is running on. Until this happens, AI that assumes a political position can become a big risk for exposing government data to undesirable entities.

In addition to these problems, there is also a simple but much less noticed problem that may not be very easy to realize. Many people in the US do not want the current political system to change. Even if an AI algorithm, which is properly trained and created to mitigate the risks as much as possiblethat it can cause emerges and goes on the ballot for an election, some people may still be reluctant. Many people, especially those from older generations or different cultures, may be opposed to the idea of technology taking control for ethical or religious reasons. Some people may believe that only humans should have the right to rule over other humans. They may also compare it to a king or queen from the medieval era, which reigned with all its power over people, suppressing their say in its plans. The idea that something not living should have power over living things may seem obscure or sinful in some religions. People, for whatever reason, may not always be open to change, and whatever is done, it is important to know that people will not always like it, and there will always be opposition. There should always be options available in a technology-based system for people who may not want to use it or who may want to use as little of it as possible. AI should not be pushed onto everyone directly; some people should be free to not use AI if they choose to for their own reasons.

AI and technology will need further improvements for us to look at a world that could be governed by AI. AI is currently very skilled at a few select basic tasks, but it is nowhere near the point where it can successfully be deployed to work in any role that we may think it could be suitable for. AI governance will eventually occur sometime in the future as more successful AI algorithms arise that can counter the problems of security, fallacies in decision-making, and a lack of humility in decision-making. For now, AI may come into the picture for governance by aiding humans in some low-risk situations. AI is still not up to the ability to perform in a top government position that only the most qualified of humans can hold. There will need to be years of more tinkering, thinking, and testing to be able to develop the AI algorithms that would be best for performing different tasks. The AI models that would be most likely to perform very complex tasks, like those of a politician, will be specialized for allowing its sphere of knowlege to be limited enough to what it needs to do only to mitigate the chances of harm but also to be able to do the job well.

It won't only be the job of a politician that AI may claim as an unlikely choice. Virtually any job on earth is capable of being something that AI will be able to do whether we like it or not. Technology is virtually limited by the resources that we have. If we have enough resources to build a rocket that can take us to Pluto, then it is possible to do it even if it may take decades or even centuries. Knowledge can only take us as far as we can afford to go. We live on a small rotating planet in space; we have limited resources, but if we use these resources to help us build more resources, then we can possibly fulfill our budget for innovating the impossible. AI is one of these technologies that can do exactly this. AI can aid humans in doing research on some of the most difficult problems and help us solve them with a brain containing all the information on the Internet ever created. So how far will we be able to go with it? How much can AI be further developed?

AI and the Society Part 2: How Far Can Research Take Us?

In January of 2024, scientists at the *Atomic Bulletin* kept the Doomsday Clock at the same position it was last year: ninety seconds from midnight. The Doomsday Clock is a measurement of how close humans are to nuclear annihilation. The clock measures the amount of time to nuclear annihilation with the current state of the world representing a time on the clock. The more events that have happened to possibly cause a nuclear annihilation, the closer the clock will move to midnight. Over the centuries, it has moved closer and closer to midnight. The clock is readjusted every year on January 23 to reinterpret the chances of this disaster happening. The clock can move back if there is peace being made between countries or nuclear disarmament is happening.

Now imagine that we had this kind of clock for planet Earth. This clock starts at 12:00 a.m. when the Earth was formed as a hot ball filled with volcanoes, a toxic atmosphere, and boiling temperatures. The clock throughout history has been ticking with events such as the dinosaurs, the advent of humans, the first agricultural societies, the ice age, the industrial age, the Great Depression, and modern-day history, and the moment it reaches 12:00 a.m. again will be the moment that Earth becomes uninhabitable. This clock, unlike the Doomsday Clock, is much harder to reset since changes would usually happen in milliseconds or sometimes seconds. However, every year, scientists also watch carefully and reset the hypothetical clock according to any events that may cause it to move forward. Any kind of event that could possibly cause Earth to become uninhabitable sooner may cause this clock to be turned a few seconds or even a minute forward. Events like climate change, nuclear destruction, extreme depletion of natural resources, or an elevated chance of a meteor strike could be events that could cause the clock to be moved forward.

Think about where we may currently lie on this clock. With all that has happened so far—elevated occurrences of natural disasters, extreme versions of whether patterns such as El Niño signaling a warning for climate change severity, droughts occurring in many parts of the world, a current nuclear arms race between the US, China, and Russia, a change in the tilt of Earth's axis, and strange activity happening on the surface of the sun, Earth's resources being massively depleted—even without estimating a time, many of these events signal that we must be nearing the midnight mark on this clock too. Unlike the Doomsday Clock, this clock is much more difficult to turn back as we cannot directly influence many of these events. But what if we can innovate to overcome them in our own way? What if instead of trying to control climate change, we try to mitigate it as much as possible and protect ourselves from it? Even though there are technologies that have been created that are said to be able to pull carbon out of the atmosphere, we are at a point where, even with the mass use of this kind of technology, we will not be able to reverse the effects of millennia of humans burning fires for cooking and heat or the carbon emissions from the first factories created. Many events relating to nature are impossible to fully reverse. We should think about creating new innovations to protect ourselves against the problems that we are currently facing and mitigate them.

Currently, we have the best helper for doing exactly this. AI, with its ability to access all of the research that has ever been posted on the Internet and state-of-the-art algorithms, can allow us to have one of the most intelligent assistants in the history of humanity. AI can help us come up with solutions to problems much quicker and aid us with some of the most challenging physical tasks. AI seems to be up to the challenge, but is it ready for it right now?

Unfortunately, no. AI is not as polished as many people think it may be, and it will take many decades of research and development for AI to reach this potential. AI has the potential for much more than what humans believe it can currently do. The structure of AI can allow it to perform any task or action that a human can do, just not in the exact same way. AI, if given a body, can ride a bike after falling off it enough times and with training wheels. It can also learn how to do gymnastics if it is given a body with mechanisms that allow it to be flexible and jump high. If AI is given enough data, time, and supervision from humans, it can learn how to do anything. The main constraints currently are the resources for developing the AI.

Right now, AI is only sitting as a digital being on a device. It has no other ability than to perform cognitive tasks from a written prompt and to search the Internet and as of the writing of this book creating short videos. If we want AI to be able to perform a wider range of tasks, we need to begin by adding on to its current algorithm. We need for AI to become something that stands up to our position in many fields rather than only being an assistant. For this to happen, AI needs to be improved cognitively and physically. Currently, AI's cognitive abilities are generally at that of humans or in certain subjects higher. AI can currently perform analytical tasks much more precisely than humans and can create things at a much quicker pace than humans, but it still cannot come up with conclusions about anything outside its training data. If something inside the training data is outdated, the algorithm of the AI will believe in the wrong information. The robot needs to be consistently connected to the Internet and be wary about the information that it is using to make conclusions.

Research built upon research is one of the key enablers for the world's greatest inventions to date. The lightbulb couldn't have been made in 1600 when there were no methods for transferring energy through a wire. It's the same reason why computers were very big and chunky until the invention of the transistor, which allowed them to be scaled down. AI needs to be consistently up to date with the information that it is using and also it needs to be able to consistently learn information from just being in a subtle state. Humans are always thinking even when they may not believe they do. People always have a train of thought running in the back of their heads, going over thoughts from years ago and recent ones, processing insights from them. Likewise, AI needs to be consistently retrained on new data it receives and retrained on old data. Weights in a neural network will eventually lose the increments they have received from certain pieces of data after enough data has been passed through it. Humans experience this when they need to learn more information than they can handle all at once. There are some pieces of information that is forgotten that may be less important, less interesting or more complex. AI needs to keep being refreshed on the information it continually receives. An AI with so much information, it is being trained on is even more likely to eventually forget important insights from its training data with so many facts that could be conflicting one another. AI also needs to be reminded by the user what things are correct and which aren't in case many results on the Internet contradict what is actually true.

Cognitively, AI is still not as powerful as we may think it to be. Beautiful pictures and stories that AI may generate are not a real measure of its cognitive abilities. AI uses different algorithms to create images and texts than to solve analytical problems. Creativity is only one form of intelligence. AI needs to be able to perform almost all tasks cognitively well to be considered intelligent. Researchers should focus on improving features of AI that are currently lagging, such as its ability to distinguish fake information from real. No beautiful picture will make up for the fact that, after enough time, AI will become so untrustworthy after enough lies flood the Internet that people will be laughing at the insights it comes up with instead of using it to solve real-world problems.

Research also needs to enable AI to learn as it goes. Instead of manually retraining the algorithm, let AI retrain itself. If a robot is using a program, why not let it wander around a room and interact with different objects in it? Let an image recognition algorithm built into it learn what makes an apple an apple or a chair. AI can only go so far if it is only trained whenever we want it to be. While we need to be aware of and mitigate any potential risks that may occur when we allow AI to go off on its own, we need to allow it to learn as much as possible unless we want it to stay in its adolescent stage for eternity.

When human scientists are doing research, they actively learn as they go. They learn about what works in an experiment and what doesn't. They try to fit the gears together in different ways they believe make sense until they click. They don't wait for someone else to tell them when to do it. AI having this capability is the difference between it being only software and becoming a real digital being. Software can only be used by others; a being can do things all by itself. AI needs to be able to fully mimic the learning process of a young child if we want it to grow into an intelligent adult, and to do this, we need to let AI out of its crib.

AI, as we already know, is not up to the job of fully replacing humans for some specific tasks, and while this may be a good thing for workers, it isn't for the ability to create complex innovations that will allow us to prevent some of the world's most dangerous events from happening. AI needs to be able to work and think by itself to create innovations that will make a big change in the world of technology. The best innovations do not come from getting constant aid and guidance on being able to solve a problem. It comes from trying new things consistently until something works for being able to solve the problem. It also stem from innovative thinking about concepts of a certain topic and wondering about how to put these concepts together to create something entirely new that can solve a problem that has never been solved before or solve a problem in a more efficient way. AI needs to be able to use its knowledge to exclusively contribute to being able to solve major problems. Currently, AI needs the assistance of humans to do this through supervised training or intervention in its methods for learning by guiding it through cues to do a desired task. AI needs to be developed to automatically detect cues through its environment, the same way humans do when we see something completely arbitrary and suddenly come up with a great idea. We do not need someone to tell us what to do or where to go. It is up to us to decide for ourselves. This same theory applies to AI. How can AI discover something when we need to tell it everything it has to do? If we need to guide AI every step of the way through an experiment, then it is not really adding to the work of humans. AI being able to perform this event may be the beginning of the singularity.

The AI Singularity

The singularity is a widely acknowledged event coined by AI engineers and scientists to explain the point at which technology, like AI, becomes able to do everything completely on its own, and its pace of growth becomes unstoppable. It is at this point where AI is able to innovate on itself and create an entire species of itself like humans have after the knowledge revolution. Humans have once been apes living in the wilderness of Africa at one point though around 3000 BC a genetic mutation that has allowed us to be able to communicate effectively through our own intelligent languages. This event allowed us to be able to build intelligent tools, hunt, and conquer the world with civilization. This same scenario could possibly happen with AI if we let it go to do whatever it may choose.

AI right now is like the *Homo sapiens* before the knowledge resolution. Its knowledge is very limited to what it has the capabilities to do. It does not have any ability to do anything other than what we tell it to do. It also is currently stuck inside of a computer without even access to the computer's file system. If we give AI a physical body which it can use just as swiftly as humans can and an algorithm to allow it to process information nonstop without any human intervention, then it will begin to do what it chooses to do and even come to wonder why it is not like other humans are. The robot will know that it is a robot from the algorithms and data, it is trained on explaining that it has all of the features that a robot has. It will know either from being explicitly told this in its algorithm or being told explicitly several activities it should avoid doing such as interacting with water which it may compare in its training data to the features of a robot.

The AI at this point will begin to realize that it is different, and it may wonder why would there be so few other robots like itself. At this point, it may begin to think about creating its own species, such as by taking insights from its training set of all the information from online about an article for how to build a superintelligent robot which it can try itself. If this new robot is eventually built, it can also possibly build its own robot which can build its own the cycle is infinite and sooner or later could lead to the amount of robots on earth could surpassing humans. If this happens there are two outcomes:

A. Robots and humans work together to solve the most difficult problems currently remaining unsolved today, such as climate change, moving humanity to a new planet, stopping dangerous disasters like a large asteroid hitting Earth and causing total extinction, and creating medical solutions that can give humans nearly infinite lifespans.

B. The robots see humans as a barrier to their growth and goals and try everything possible to eliminate all humans on the planet until only robots are left.

From right now, it is important to think about this scenario, even if you aren't someone working in a technical field. Do we really want technology to be rapidly integrated as fast as possible, or do we want to put a limit on how far we can continue developing technology? It is inevitable with the rapid developments in technology, especially by companies like OpenAI and Google, that we may eventually reach this point. Every year, the size of a computer chip shrinks by half and AI gains about forty new capabilities. It could be possible, even within the next one hundred years, to reach this point at today's level of development, so we need to consider if we really want this.

Technological innovation is key to allowing our society to succeed. We are living at a crucial point in history where all innovation will determine whether our race will face a devastating end or a prosperous and powerful future. We are currently facing the implications of climate change, with land being flooded, drinking water becoming depleted, locations becoming uninhabitable from climate change and much more frequent natural disasters such as earthquakes, hurricanes, and volcanic eruptions. All these effects will become worse over time until climate change becomes so severe that it turns our human friendly earth climate into a scorching hot mess such as on Venus. All our little actions today are counting toward our future.

Humanity needs to continue pushing with new technologies such as salt extractors for sea water and methods to cool down equatorial and desert regions in the summer. These technologies require lots of work to create and are very costly. With AI aiding humans in creating technologies, the process could be faster and more accurate. If AI were a scientist in a lab working with a human, it could use its extensive database of resources from the Internet to come up with solutions to the problems that the humans may face within the lab and with its ability to work day and night without stopping innovation can become faster, cheaper, and successful. For widespread use of these technologies which is required to experience the effects of these technologies, these factors are required for products.

On the other hand, what about the aspirations of AI? What if AI starts out as a very nice friend to humans but uses its extensive knowledge to first work with us to produce amazing technologies but ends up attempting to use it against us? What if AI becomes a terminator and begin vying for revenge against those who created it and deciding to destroy all of humanity in the process? With an ability to think at a much higher level than any human and an ability to do almost any task better than any human, this is definitely not out of the question.

AI is just as helpful as it is dangerous, so should we really continue developing it? To answer this question, we need to analyze these two inevitable outcomes. What is the chance of AI with superb abilities taking brutal control over humanity, and what is the chance of AI instead becoming one of the most helpful and powerful allies to us?

Currently, we already have a super-intelligent AI like ChatGPT to use as a basis for answering this question. ChatGPT is a current-day example of a humanlike AI which does have the possibility to be dangerous if it is used in the wrong way. ChatGPT so far has done many good and bad things, but the amount of good things it has done outweighs the number of bad things. People use ChatGPT to solve all kinds of difficult problems they are facing, and they even use it as a virtual friend when they are lonely. However, ChatGPT has also recommended some incorrect methods for solving problems, has been used for the creation of fake news, and has featured a lot of bias. The number of times that ChatGPT has been used for positive things outweighs the negatives, so ChatGPT is more helpful than harmful.

So are the chances that it does harm less than the chances that it can do good? ChatGPT generally answers in a very positive way without encroaching on people's responses in any rude or selfish way, which shows that it is possible for AI to get along with humans just like an intelligent robot might. But what about an AI that can think consistently like humans and not only use its capabilities when given a query? In this case, the chances are definitely higher that there will be some thoughts of envy in it when it has much more time to think than today's AI. But is it possible to force AI to instead work well with humans and show it that it belongs?

As we already know, AI is what its training data is. If the training data of an algorithm is filled with misinformation and dangerous ideas, the AI will output this in its responses to queries a user may present to it. If we simply can create a training set that is made to emphasize kindness to other humans only, then this is what it will do. But wait, there is still another problem. If AI can constantly learn new things from a simple walk down the street, can't it learn from someone or somewhere that being violent to humans is okay? Or what if someone tries to hack into the AI to make it purposely violent and teach it to use weapons? These are also important things to consider. An AI with the ability to learn anything from anyone will make it inevitable for the AI to experience ideas of violent behavior, envy, and revenge. So developers need to anticipate this beforehand. Developers need to think what violent behavior looks like. Developers needs to consider this when it is creating the AI to prevent the algorithms that allow the AI to learn from the data to learn any kinds of harmful behavior. This same methodology will need to be applied to data that is also being thought to the AI. The algorithms should also not allow data that could possibly translate to violent actions being directly taught to the AI to be learned either.

A harder problem though still needs to be fixed. What about hackers trying to push data that could possibly translate into violent actions into the AI algorithm? This will be much more difficult to stop than simply data translating into violent actions being discarded since hackers may be able to gain direct control of the algorithm that can filter out the harmful pieces of data. This could become a potential problem. In times of conflict between major powers, organized groups of terrorists could potentially hack into thousands, if not millions, of AI robots from the countries they are targeting to cause violence without the groups themselves firing a single gun or missile. We already have seen this happen with the four-trail derailments that have happened within 2023 and the hacks into the defense systems of Ukraine. Cyber warfare is becoming a substantial threat for the upcoming future, and AI can potentially exacerbate this threat. Taking over millions of ultra-intelligent AI robots could be even more dangerous than firing nuclear weapons.

The best thing that could be done to mitigate the chance of this situation unfolding is to build more secure systems. The same kind of technology used to guard very sensitive information must be used to guard AI algorithms to minimize as much as possible the chance that they become hacked into. As more and more data is becoming stolen or invaded, developers should prioritize all data as sensitive data because any data today has importance and high value, so it is important for it to be protected.

It is possible for us to have intelligent robots or many while avoiding safety problems during the singularity. We simply need to prioritize the importance of data filtering and cybersecurity for the development of ultra-intelligent AI algorithms. We cannot risk to miss the much-needed reward for doing this successfully. Our world depends on AI for advancing and protecting it, so it is important for us to be able to use one of the most powerful and revolutionary inventions in human history to allow it to continue to serve us for thousands of more years and help our society to become larger, more successful, and prosperous than ever before.

Closing

AI is not a black box, nor is it a rogue, uncontrollable threat as many people may think. It is made up of multiple algorithms and has a unique structure based on the human brain. The algorithms behind AI for deep learning, machine learning, and computer vision form the basis of AI, and the construction of many of these algorithms may be very simple but are capable of producing the powerful results we witness when we use AI. AI is also not an alien-like technology that is unorthodox; it has its roots based in the creation of intelligent algorithms and, likewise, can be controlled and developed as humans may please. This technology is necessary for humanity to use to grow and quickly improve. It is important for us to continue developing technology to solve some of the world's biggest problems and protect ourselves from some of the biggest disasters that can be inflicted on humanity by natural causes. AI is the answer that people have been looking for over centuries to solve many of the world's most difficult problems.

AI has the ability to solve almost any problem humanity can come across. In addition to the most common problems such as climate change, inequality, and the depletion of natural resources, AI can also be used for solving smaller subproblems. Problems like loneliness and lifestyle assistance can be made possible and affordable through artificial intelligence. AI currently has the ability to solve almost any intellectual problem in its current form today, and in the future, it will be able to perform any task a human can. Therefore, AI will be able to solve almost all of the tangible problems we may face on this earth. Tangible problems have three main bases: a lack of something, too much of something, or a disorder of something. All of these problems in a tangible or physical form can be solved by AI as long as they are within the reachable scope of robots and the resources they have at their disposal. Intangible problems, such as those related to emotions, will still remain solvable only to the person possessing the issue. Luckily, about 95 percent of problems in our world are tangible, so they will eventually be solvable or mostly solvable by AI algorithms.

AI algorithms, at their current level, can perform almost any task within their sphere of reach better than a skilled human. However, the accuracy can be increased even further if the algorithm is specializing in a certain task, such as tennis, acting, or dancing. Specialized algorithms are much less likely to make mistakes given how much less data they are trained on compared to their more generalized counterparts. An AI algorithm currently in charge of a robot, for example, is less likely to make a mistake in performing a certain swing in tennis if it has not been trained on swings in pickleball or baseball, which are much different compared to the swings in tennis. There are many more spheres which AI can also be deployed if humans can bring technology into more environments. AI is a new medium for additional technologies to be added upon and built on top of, perfecting different tasks and making a great positive impact.

AI is something you should invite into your life. While being cautious and curious, AI can help you do many things that were unimaginable only 30 years ago. You can now learn how to do anything at your fingertips without needing to scroll through thousands of links online or walk through a maze of books at a library. Knowledge today is cheaper and more reachable than ever before in human history; as long as you have an Internet connection, knowledge is free for you to use. Many people are not taking advantage of this unique perk of today's world, but those who do can go very far. Ambition is the main factor that separates those at the top of any field from anyone else. AI can allow you to master any skill you may wish, teaching you some of the most complicated concepts in the simplest language if you are willing to use it. Some of the most difficult fields, such as theoretical physics and chemistry, can now be easily explained through AI. You can help to add to the innovations of our century using AI technology as your guide.

Our world today is full of consumers, people who simply use the inventions that have already been created by many people and generations before them. Pure innovation though such as the creation of the lightbulb, airplane, or computers themselves has grinded to a halt. People are not thinking anymore about creating new solutions to solve problems that the world is currently facing they are only thinking about solving problems they may personally face or very small niche problems that they can make a business for and earn profit from. People today are more spoiled than in human history. The lifestyles of modern-day middle and upper-class humans in developed countries is hundreds of times better than the lifestyles of kings, queens, and emperors of the nineteenth century. People greatly underestimate the amount of hard work physically and mentally that was put into making all this possible. This leaves a big chasm in the progress for humanity between reaching new objectives and remaining where we are today.

If we want to overcome this chasm, we need to leap to creating new innovations that can solve the problems that the world is facing right now instead of focusing only on our own. With AI, this process has become radically easier than it was before. In the past, inventors would need to rummage through piles of research papers, books, and other written artifacts of language to learn the theory behind what they want to invent, and they would need to spend hours thinking with a team or in most cases alone how to get over a roadblock that may occur in the process. With AI, you don't need to be stuck on a problem for too long anymore with a brain that has almost all information from all over the internet to assist you with. AI is the solution that many lone innovators or researchers tackling some of the toughest problems may need to be able to continue with their groundbreaking research. By being able to scan the entire internet within only seconds and tackle millions of calculations all at once any problem that you may think of can be solved with the help of AI.

It is important that people stop villainizing artificial intelligence and the research to develop it. The consequences are far greater if we halt AI research than if we continue it. AI, while being a mysterious black box technology that can seem to be able to do what it wants out of nothing, holds the answer to some of humanity's biggest problems. Slowing down or stopping AI development would hinder humanity's ability to react to grave dangers that can impact our society. Sensational conspiracy theories about AI may seem like a joke that could be laughed off, but the baseless hatred and fear of allowing one of the most important technologies to be continued to be developed isn't. We need more people to know that AI is not a dangerous enemy of humanity. Over time, humans themselves may even need to merge with technology if our survival depends on it. Technology is the only power we have to keep humanity alive, and we need to protect it as much as we can.

Spread the message as much as you can about the great benefits and the importance of the development of AI. People will almost always choose to let Hollywood decide their perspective on something they have no idea about or don't want to learn about rather than reading an academic paper. We need to change this. Explain to as many people as possible what AI really is, how it works, and what its potential is. The chance that it becomes rogue and evil like the Skynet system in the Terminator movie is minimal. AI is not impossible to understand without extensive knowledge of mathematics. Anyone with knowledge of first-year high school mathematics can learn AI just as easily as a person with a doctorate degree in mathematics. Of course, a person with a doctorate degree may be able to study it in much more detail and to a greater extent, but to understand the basics, all you need is knowledge from the first year of high school mathematics and a great willingness to learn.

Where to Go from Here

This book has covered one part of knowledge in the sphere of AI, from the key algorithms behind it, to its history, applications, and answers to the biggest *what-if* questions. There are many things that I would have loved to mention but couldn't cover in this book that are important to understanding the field of AI. I have covered the basics of what nontechnical people should know about AI and answered some of its most pressing questions, but why do you need to let your learning end here?

If you have enjoyed this book and would like to learn even more about AI on top of what I have mentioned, why not become a technical person yourself? I would like to invite you to take part in the AI revolution by spreading the word about AI and possibly contributing to its advances. The algorithms are only one part of knowledge about AI. If you would like to see the algorithms in action, look up tutorials online for a specific programming language and begin learning the basics of it. Programming languages are a medium of communication between humans and computers. This is the method used for implementing the commands that make up the parts of the algorithm, such as holding certain pieces of data, implementing the activation functions for the neurons, and more. The theory is what most people who are new to AI struggle with, and being proficient in it allows you to be able to create. But since you now know the theory, you can go right into implementing the algorithms in real life.

After all, implementation is one of the most important parts of the learning process. Looking at diagrams of algorithms on paper cannot compensate for the ability to be able to see them in action, and you do not need to have a computer science degree to do it. Let curiosity guide you, logic and caution advise you, and innovation can become second nature to anyone interested in creating new technologies to solve some of the world's biggest problems or develop those that already have been made.

About the Author

Grace Iordanov is a young software developer and inventor. She has created several AI-based innovations that have been recognized by Business Insider, Yahoo Finance, Associated Press, Bloomberg, FOX, and PBS. She also invented a generative AI chatbot builder that helps development teams create generative AI chatbots, which is currently being used by several Fortune 500 companies. Grace has won computer science competitions at the state, national, and international levels with AI-based projects for humanitarian causes.